Cloudera Administration Handbook

A complete, hands-on guide to building and maintaining large Apache Hadoop clusters using Cloudera Manager and CDH5

Rohit Menon

PUBLISHING

BIRMINGHAM - MUMBAI

Cloudera Administration Handbook

First published: July 2014

Production reference: 1110714

Published by Packt Publishing Ltd.
Livery Place
35 Livery Street
Birmingham B3 2PB, UK.

ISBN 978-1-78355-896-4

www.packtpub.com

Cover image by John Michael Harkness (jtothem@gmail.com)

Credits

Author
Rohit Menon

Reviewers
Skanda Bhargav

Brandon Forehand

Mike Hordila

Commissioning Editor
Akram Hussain

Acquisition Editor
Gregory Wild

Content Development Editor
Priya Singh

Technical Editors
Kunal Anil Gaikwad

Edwin Moses

Siddhi Rane

Copy Editors
Janbal Dharmaraj

Deepa Nambiar

Alfida Paiva

Laxmi Subramanian

Project Coordinators
Swati Kumari

Amey Sawant

Proofreaders
Simran Bhogal

Ameesha Green

Maria Gould

Indexer
Rekha Nair

Graphics
Disha Haria

Production Coordinator
Nitesh Thakur

Cover Work
Nitesh Thakur

About the Author

Rohit Menon is a senior system analyst living in Denver, Colorado. He has over 7 years of experience in the field of Information Technology, which started with the role of a real-time applications developer back in 2006. He now works for a product-based company specializing in software for large telecom operators.

He graduated with a master's degree in Computer Applications from University of Pune, where he built an autonomous maze-solving robot as his final year project. He later joined a software consulting company in India where he worked on C#, SQL Server, C++, and RTOS to provide software solutions to reputable organizations in USA and Japan. After this, he started working for a product-based company where most of his time was dedicated to programming the finer details of products using C++, Oracle, Linux, and Java.

He is a person who always likes to learn new technologies and this got him interested in web application development. He picked up Ruby, Ruby on Rails, HTML, JavaScript, CSS, and built `www.flicksery.com`, a Netflix search engine that makes searching for titles on Netflix much easier.

On the Hadoop front, he is a Cloudera Certified Apache Hadoop Developer. He blogs at `www.rohitmenon.com`, mainly on topics related to Apache Hadoop and its components. To share his learning, he has also started `www.hadoopscreencasts.com`, a website that teaches Apache Hadoop using simple, short, and easy-to-follow screencasts. He is well versed with wide variety of tools and techniques such as MapReduce, Hive, Pig, Sqoop, Oozie, and Talend Open Studio.

I would like to thank my parents for instilling the qualities of perseverance and hard work. I would also like to thank my wife, Madhuri, and my daughter, Anushka, for being patient and allowing me to spend most of my time studying and researching.

About the Reviewers

Skanda Bhargav is an engineering graduate from Visvesvaraya Technological University (VTU), Belgaum in Karnataka, India. He did his majors in Computer Science Engineering. He is currently employed with Happiest Minds Technologies, a MNC based out of Bangalore. He is a Cloudera Certified Developer for Apache Hadoop. His interests are Big Data and Hadoop.

He has been a reviewer for the following books:

- *Instant MapReduce Patterns – Hadoop Essentials How-to, Srinath Perera, Packt Publishing*
- *Hadoop Cluster Deployment, Danil Zburivsky, Packt Publishing*

He has also reviewed *Building Hadoop Clusters [Video], Sean Mikha, Packt Publishing*.

I would like to thank my family for their immense support and faith in me throughout my learning stage. My friends have brought the confidence in me to a level that makes me bring out the best out of myself. I am happy that God has blessed me with such wonderful people around me, without which this work might not have been the success that it is today.

Brandon Forehand started programming at an early age and loves solving problems. He is a Cloudera Certified Apache Hadoop Developer and currently works at Moz as a principal software engineer on the Big Data team, developing systems to index links on the web and providing data to help online marketers improve their websites' visibility. Previously, he worked at Amazon on Kindle and developed software to convert physical books to e-books. He has also worked at a research laboratory, developing sonar systems for the Navy. He earned a BSc in Computer Science from the University of Texas, Austin.

I would like to thank my wife for putting up with me all of these years and the countless people who have helped me along the way in my career.

Mike Hordila has worked with very large databases and high availability systems for more than 20 years. He consults for major organizations, always looking for new ways and technologies. He has shared some of his experience in a number of articles in major Oracle magazines and also in a couple of books.

www.PacktPub.com

Support files, eBooks, discount offers, and more

You might want to visit www.PacktPub.com for support files and downloads related to your book.

Did you know that Packt offers eBook versions of every book published, with PDF and ePub files available? You can upgrade to the eBook version at www.PacktPub.com and as a print book customer, you are entitled to a discount on the eBook copy. Get in touch with us at service@packtpub.com for more details.

At www.PacktPub.com, you can also read a collection of free technical articles, sign up for a range of free newsletters, and receive exclusive discounts and offers on Packt books and eBooks.

http://PacktLib.PacktPub.com

Do you need instant solutions to your IT questions? PacktLib is Packt's online digital book library. Here, you can access, read, and search across Packt's entire library of books.

Why subscribe?

- Fully searchable across every book published by Packt
- Copy and paste, print, and bookmark content
- On demand and accessible via web browser

Free access for Packt account holders

If you have an account with Packt at www.PacktPub.com, you can use this to access PacktLib today and view nine entirely free books. Simply use your login credentials for immediate access.

Table of Contents

Preface

Apache Hadoop is an open source distributed computing technology that assists users in processing large volumes of data with relative ease, helping them to generate tremendous insights into their data. Cloudera, with their open source distribution of Hadoop, has made data analytics on Big Data possible and accessible to anyone interested.

This book fully prepares you to be a Hadoop administrator, with special emphasis on Cloudera. It provides step-by-step instructions on setting up and managing a robust Hadoop cluster running Cloudera's Distribution Including Apache Hadoop (CDH).

This book starts out by giving you a brief introduction to Apache Hadoop and Cloudera. You will then move on to learn about all the tools and techniques needed to set up and manage a production-standard Hadoop cluster using CDH and Cloudera Manager.

In this book, you will learn the Hadoop architecture by understanding the different features of HDFS and walking through the entire flow of a MapReduce process. With this understanding, you will start exploring the different applications packaged into CDH and will follow a step-by-step guide to set up HDFS High Availability (HA) and HDFS Federation.

You will learn to use Cloudera Manager, Cloudera's cluster management application. Using Cloudera Manager, you will walk through the steps to configure security using Kerberos, learn about events and alerts, and also configure backups.

What this book covers

Chapter 1, Getting Started with Apache Hadoop, introduces you to Apache Hadoop and walks you through the different Apache Hadoop daemons.

Chapter 2, HDFS and MapReduce, provides you with an in-depth understanding of HDFS and MapReduce.

Chapter 3, Cloudera's Distribution Including Apache Hadoop, introduces you to Cloudera's Apache Hadoop Distribution and walks you through its installation steps.

Chapter 4, Exploring HDFS Federation and Its High Availability, introduces you to the steps to configure a federated HDFS and also provides step-by-step instructions to set up HDFS High Availability.

Chapter 5, Using Cloudera Manager, introduces you to Cloudera Manager, Cloudera's cluster management application and walks you through the steps to install Cloudera Manager.

Chapter 6, Implementing Security Using Kerberos, walks you through the steps to secure your cluster by configuring Kerberos.

Chapter 7, Managing an Apache Hadoop Cluster, introduces you to all the cluster management capabilities available within Cloudera Manager.

Chapter 8, Cluster *Monitoring Using Events and Alerts*, introduces you to the different events and alerts available within Cloudera Manager that will assist you in monitoring your cluster effectively.

Chapter 9, Configuring Backups, walks you through the steps to configure backups and snapshots using Cloudera Manager.

What you need for this book

You will need access to a cluster of around three to four nodes (physical server or virtual machines) running Linux, preferably the CentOS distribution. The steps to acquire the software needed is explained in detail in this book.

Who this book is for

This book is ideal for anyone interested in administering an Apache Hadoop cluster. This book will prove to be a good guide for administrators managing clusters running Cloudera's Distribution Including Apache Hadoop (CDH) and will be introduced to the various tools and techniques such as cluster management, security, monitoring, and backups. The reader will acquire all the knowledge required to run production scale clusters ranging from a few nodes to thousands of nodes.

Conventions

In this book, you will find a number of styles of text that distinguish between different kinds of information. Here are some examples of these styles, and an explanation of their meaning.

Code words in text, database table names, folder names, filenames, file extensions, pathnames, dummy URLs, user input, and Twitter handles are shown as follows: "It is important to note that the `fsimage` file is not updated for every write operation."

A block of code is set as follows:

```
<property>
  <name>dfs.namenode.servicerpc-address</name>
  <value>node1.hcluster:8022</value>
</property>
```

Any command-line input or output is written as follows:

```
$ sudo yum install flume-ng
$ sudo yum install flume-ng-agent
```

New terms and **important words** are shown in bold. Words that you see on the screen, in menus or dialog boxes for example, appear in the text like this: "The **Coordinators** tab lists all the coordinator applications that have been configured in Oozie."

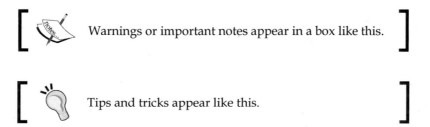

Warnings or important notes appear in a box like this.

Tips and tricks appear like this.

Reader feedback

Feedback from our readers is always welcome. Let us know what you think about this book—what you liked or may have disliked. Reader feedback is important for us to develop titles that you really get the most out of.

To send us general feedback, simply send an e-mail to feedback@packtpub.com, and mention the book title via the subject of your message.

If there is a topic that you have expertise in and you are interested in either writing or contributing to a book, see our author guide on www.packtpub.com/authors.

Customer support

Now that you are the proud owner of a Packt book, we have a number of things to help you to get the most from your purchase.

Downloading the example code

You can download the example code files for all Packt books you have purchased from your account at http://www.packtpub.com. If you purchased this book elsewhere, you can visit http://www.packtpub.com/support and register to have the files e-mailed directly to you.

Errata

Although we have taken every care to ensure the accuracy of our content, mistakes do happen. If you find a mistake in one of our books—maybe a mistake in the text or the code—we would be grateful if you would report this to us. By doing so, you can save other readers from frustration and help us improve subsequent versions of this book. If you find any errata, please report them by visiting http://www.packtpub.com/submit-errata, selecting your book, clicking on the **errata submission form** link, and entering the details of your errata. Once your errata are verified, your submission will be accepted and the errata will be uploaded on our website, or added to any list of existing errata, under the Errata section of that title. Any existing errata can be viewed by selecting your title from http://www.packtpub.com/support.

Piracy

Piracy of copyright material on the Internet is an ongoing problem across all media. At Packt, we take the protection of our copyright and licenses very seriously. If you come across any illegal copies of our works, in any form, on the Internet, please provide us with the location address or website name immediately so that we can pursue a remedy.

Please contact us at copyright@packtpub.com with a link to the suspected pirated material.

We appreciate your help in protecting our authors, and our ability to bring you valuable content.

Questions

You can contact us at questions@packtpub.com if you are having a problem with any aspect of the book, and we will do our best to address it.

1
Getting Started with Apache Hadoop

Apache Hadoop is a widely used open source distributed computing framework that is employed to efficiently process large volumes of data using large clusters of cheap or commodity computers. In this chapter, we will learn more about Apache Hadoop by covering the following topics:

- History of Apache Hadoop and its trends
- Components of Apache Hadoop
- Understanding the Apache Hadoop daemons
- Introducing Cloudera
- What is CDH?
- Responsibilities of a Hadoop administrator

History of Apache Hadoop and its trends

We live in the era where almost everything surrounding us is generating some kind of data. A click on a web page is being logged on the server. The flipping of channels when watching TV is being captured by cable companies. A search on a search engine is being logged. A heartbeat of a patient in a hospital generates data. A single phone call generates data, which is stored and maintained by telecom companies. An order of pizza generates data. It is very difficult to find processes these days that don't generate and store data.

Why would any organization want to store data? The present and the future belongs to those who hold onto their data and work with it to improve their current operations and innovate to generate newer products and opportunities. Data and the creative use of it is the heart of organizations such as Google, Facebook, Netflix, Amazon, and Yahoo!. They have proven that data, along with powerful analysis, helps in building fantastic and powerful products.

Organizations have been storing data for several years now. However, the data remained on backup tapes or drives. Once it has been archived on storage devices such as tapes, it can only be used in case of emergency to retrieve important data. However, processing or analyzing this data to get insight efficiently is very difficult. This is changing. Organizations want to now use this data to get insight to help understand existing problems, seize new opportunities, and be more profitable. The study and analysis of these vast volumes of data has given birth to a term called **big data**. It is a phrase often used to promote the importance of the ever-growing data and the technologies applied to analyze this data.

Big and small companies now understand the importance of data and are adding loggers to their operations with an intention to generate more data every day. This has given rise to a very important problem—storage and efficient retrieval of data for analysis. With the data growing at such a rapid rate, traditional tools for storage and analysis fall short. Though these days the cost per byte has reduced considerably and the ability to store more data has increased, the disk transfer rate has remained the same. This has been a bottleneck for processing large volumes of data. Data in many organizations have reached petabytes and is continuing to grow. Several companies have been working to solve this problem and have come out with a few commercial offerings that leverage the power of distributed computing. In this solution, multiple computers work together (a **cluster**) to store and process large volumes of data in parallel, thus making the analysis of large volumes of data possible. Google, the Internet search engine giant, ran into issues when their data, acquired by crawling the Web, started growing to such large volumes that it was getting increasingly impossible to process. They had to find a way to solve this problem and this led to the creation of **Google File System (GFS)** and **MapReduce**.

The GFS or GoogleFS is a filesystem created by Google that enables them to store their large amount of data easily across multiple nodes in a cluster. Once stored, they use MapReduce, a programming model developed by Google to process (or query) the data stored in GFS efficiently. The MapReduce programming model implements a parallel, distributed algorithm on the cluster, where the processing goes to the location where data resides, making it faster to generate results rather than wait for the data to be moved to the processing, which could be a very time consuming activity. Google found tremendous success using this architecture and released white papers for GFS in 2003 and MapReduce in 2004.

Around 2002, Doug Cutting and Mike Cafarella were working on Nutch, an open source web search engine, and faced problems of scalability when trying to store billions of web pages that were crawled everyday by Nutch. In 2004, the Nutch team discovered that the GFS architecture was the solution to their problem and started working on an implementation based on the GFS white paper. They called their filesystem **Nutch Distributed File System (NDFS)**. In 2005, they also implemented MapReduce for NDFS based on Google's MapReduce white paper.

In 2006, the Nutch team realized that their implementations, NDFS and MapReduce, could be applied to more areas and could solve the problems of large data volume processing. This led to the formation of a project called Hadoop. Under Hadoop, NDFS was renamed to **Hadoop Distributed File System (HDFS)**. After Doug Cutting joined Yahoo! in 2006, Hadoop received lot of attention within Yahoo!, and Hadoop became a very important system running successfully on top of a very large cluster (around 1000 nodes). In 2008, Hadoop became one of Apache's top-level projects.

So, Apache Hadoop is a framework written in Java that:

- Is used for distributed storage and processing of large volumes of data, which run on top of a cluster and can scale from a single computer to thousands of computers

- Uses the MapReduce programming model to process data

- Stores and processes data on every worker node (the nodes on the cluster that are responsible for the storage and processing of data) and handles hardware failures efficiently, providing high availability

Apache Hadoop has made distributed computing accessible to anyone who wants to try and process their large volumes of data without shelling out big bucks to commercial offerings. The success of Apache Hadoop implementations in organizations such as Facebook, Netflix, LinkedIn, Twitter, The New York Times, and many more have given the much deserved recognition to Apache Hadoop and in turn good confidence to other organizations to make it a core part of their system. Having made large data analysis a possibility, Hadoop has also given rise to many startups that build analytics products on top of Apache Hadoop.

Components of Apache Hadoop

Apache Hadoop is composed of two core components. They are:

- **HDFS**: The HDFS is responsible for the storage of files. It is the storage component of Apache Hadoop, which was designed and developed to handle large files efficiently. It is a distributed filesystem designed to work on a cluster and makes it easy to store large files by splitting the files into blocks and distributing them across multiple nodes redundantly. The users of HDFS need not worry about the underlying networking aspects, as HDFS takes care of it. HDFS is written in Java and is a filesystem that runs within the user space.

- **MapReduce**: MapReduce is a programming model that was built from models found in the field of functional programming and distributed computing. In MapReduce, the task is broken down to two parts: **map** and **reduce**. All data in MapReduce flows in the form of key and value pairs, `<key, value>`. Mappers emit key and value pairs and the reducers receive them, work on them, and produce the final result. This model was specifically built to query/process the large volumes of data stored in HDFS.

We will be going through HDFS and MapReduce in depth in the next chapter.

Understanding the Apache Hadoop daemons

Most of the Apache Hadoop clusters in production run Apache Hadoop 1.x (MRv1 — MapReduce Version 1). However, the new version of Apache Hadoop, 2.x (MRv2 — MapReduce Version 2), also referred to as **Yet Another Resource Negotiator (YARN)** is being adopted by many organizations actively. In this section, we shall go through the daemons for both these versions.

Apache Hadoop 1.x (MRv1) consists of the following daemons:

- Namenode
- Secondary namenode
- Jobtracker
- Datanode
- Tasktracker

All the preceding daemons are Java services and run within their own JVM.

Apache Hadoop stores and processes data in a distributed fashion. To achieve this goal, Hadoop implements a master and slave model. The namenode and jobtracker daemons are master daemons, whereas the datanode and tasktracker daemons are slave daemons.

Namenode

The **namenode** daemon is a master daemon and is responsible for storing all the location information of the files present in HDFS. The actual data is never stored on a namenode. In other words, it holds the metadata of the files in HDFS.

The namenode maintains the entire metadata in RAM, which helps clients receive quick responses to read requests. Therefore, it is important to run namenode from a machine that has lots of RAM at its disposal. The higher the number of files in HDFS, the higher the consumption of RAM. The namenode daemon also maintains a persistent checkpoint of the metadata in a file stored on the disk called the fsimage file.

Whenever a file is placed/deleted/updated in the cluster, an entry of this action is updated in a file called the edits logfile. After updating the edits log, the metadata present in-memory is also updated accordingly. It is important to note that the fsimage file is not updated for every write operation.

In case the namenode daemon is restarted, the following sequence of events occur at namenode boot up:

1. Read the fsimage file from the disk and load it into memory (RAM).
2. Read the actions that are present in the edits log and apply each action to the in-memory representation of the fsimage file.
3. Write the modified in-memory representation to the fsimage file on the disk.

The preceding steps make sure that the in-memory representation is up to date.

The namenode daemon is a single point of failure in Hadoop 1.x, which means that if the node hosting the namenode daemon fails, the filesystem becomes unusable. To handle this, the administrator has to configure the namenode to write the fsimage file to the local disk as well as a remote disk on the network. This backup on the remote disk can be used to restore the namenode on a freshly installed server. Newer versions of Apache Hadoop (2.x) now support **High Availability (HA)**, which deploys two namenodes in an active/passive configuration, wherein if the active namenode fails, the control falls onto the passive namenode, making it active. This configuration reduces the downtime in case of a namenode failure.

Since the `fsimage` file is not updated for every operation, it is possible the `edits` logfile would grow to a very large file. The restart of namenode service would become very slow because all the actions in the large `edits` logfile will have to be applied on the `fsimage` file. The slow boot up time could be avoided using the secondary namenode daemon.

Secondary namenode

The **secondary namenode** daemon is responsible for performing periodic housekeeping functions for namenode. It only creates checkpoints of the filesystem metadata (`fsimage`) present in namenode by merging the `edits` logfile and the `fsimage` file from the namenode daemon. In case the namenode daemon fails, this checkpoint could be used to rebuild the filesystem metadata. However, it is important to note that checkpoints are done in intervals and it is possible that the checkpoint data could be slightly outdated. Rebuilding the `fsimage` file using such a checkpoint could lead to data loss. The secondary namenode is not a failover node for the namenode daemon.

It is recommended that the secondary namenode daemon be hosted on a separate machine for large clusters. The checkpoints are created by merging the `edits` logfiles and the `fsimage` file from the namenode daemon.

The following are the steps carried out by the secondary namenode daemon:

1. Get the `edits` logfile from the primary namenode daemon.
2. Get the `fsimage` file from the primary namenode daemon.
3. Apply all the actions present in the `edits` logs to the `fsimage` file.
4. Push the `fsimage` file back to the primary namenode.

This is done periodically and so whenever the namenode daemon is restarted, it would have a relatively updated version of the `fsimage` file and the boot up time would be significantly faster. The following diagram shows the communication between namenode and secondary namenode:

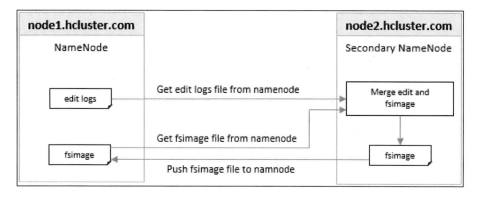

The **datanode** daemon acts as a slave node and is responsible for storing the actual files in HDFS. The files are split as data blocks across the cluster. The blocks are typically 64 MB to 128 MB size blocks. The block size is a configurable parameter. The file blocks in a Hadoop cluster also replicate themselves to other datanodes for redundancy so that no data is lost in case a datanode daemon fails. The datanode daemon sends information to the namenode daemon about the files and blocks stored in that node and responds to the namenode daemon for all filesystem operations. The following diagram shows how files are stored in the cluster:

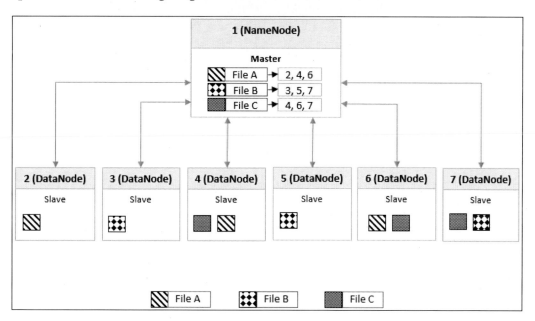

File blocks of files A, B, and C are replicated across multiple nodes of the cluster for redundancy. This ensures availability of data even if one of the nodes fail. You can also see that blocks of file A are present on nodes 2, 4, and 6; blocks of file B are present on nodes 3, 5, and 7; and blocks of file C are present on 4, 6, and 7. The replication factor configured for this cluster is 3, which signifies that each file block is replicated three times across the cluster. It is the responsibility of the namenode daemon to maintain a list of the files and their corresponding locations on the cluster. Whenever a client needs to access a file, the namenode daemon provides the location of the file to client and the client, then accesses the file directly from the datanode daemon.

Jobtracker

The **jobtracker** daemon is responsible for accepting job requests from a client and scheduling/assigning tasktrackers with tasks to be performed. The jobtracker daemon tries to assign tasks to the tasktracker daemon on the datanode daemon where the data to be processed is stored. This feature is called **data locality**. If that is not possible, it will at least try to assign tasks to tasktrackers within the same physical server rack. If for some reason the node hosting the datanode and tasktracker daemons fails, the jobtracker daemon assigns the task to another tasktracker daemon where the replica of the data exists. This is possible because of the replication factor configuration for HDFS where the data blocks are replicated across multiple datanodes. This ensures that the job does not fail even if a node fails within the cluster.

Tasktracker

The **tasktracker** daemon is a daemon that accepts tasks (map, reduce, and shuffle) from the jobtracker daemon. The tasktracker daemon is the daemon that performs the actual tasks during a MapReduce operation. The tasktracker daemon sends a heartbeat message to jobtracker, periodically, to notify the jobtracker daemon that it is alive. Along with the heartbeat, it also sends the free slots available within it, to process tasks. The tasktracker daemon starts and monitors the map, and reduces tasks and sends progress/status information back to the jobtracker daemon.

In small clusters, the namenode and jobtracker daemons reside on the same node. However, in larger clusters, there are dedicated nodes for the namenode and jobtracker daemons. This can be easily understood from the following diagram:

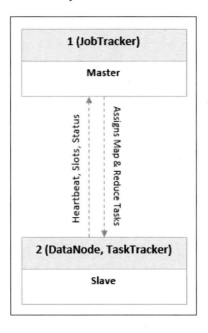

In a Hadoop cluster, these daemons can be monitored via specific URLs using a browser. The specific URLs are of the `http://<serveraddress>:port_number` type.

By default, the ports for the Hadoop daemons are:

The Hadoop daemon	Port
Namenode	50070
Secondary namenode	50090
Jobtracker	50030
Datanode	50075
Tasktracker	50060

The preceding mentioned ports can be configured in the `hdfs-site.xml` and `mapred-site.xml` files.

YARN is a general-purpose, distributed, application management framework for processing data in Hadoop clusters.

YARN was built to solve the following two important problems:

- Support for large clusters (4000 nodes or more)
- The ability to run other applications apart from MapReduce to make use of data already stored in HDFS, for example, MPI and Apache Giraph

In Hadoop Version 1.x, MapReduce can be divided into the following two parts:

- **The MapReduce user framework**: This consists of the user's interaction with MapReduce such as the application programming interface for MapReduce
- **The MapReduce system**: This consists of system level tasks such as monitoring, scheduling, and restarting of failed tasks

The jobtracker daemon had these two parts tightly coupled within itself and was responsible for managing the tasks and all its related operations by interacting with the tasktracker daemon. This responsibility turned out to be overwhelming for the jobtracker daemon when the nodes in the cluster started increasing and reached the 4000 node mark. This was a scalability issue that needed to be fixed. Also, the investment in Hadoop could not be justified as MapReduce was the only way to process data on HDFS. Other tools were unable to process this data. YARN was built to address these issues and is part of Hadoop Version 2.x. With the introduction of YARN, MapReduce is now just one of the clients that run on the YARN framework.

YARN addresses the preceding mentioned issues by splitting the following two jobtracker responsibilities:

- Resource management
- Job scheduling/monitoring

The jobtracker daemon has been removed and the following two new daemons have been introduced in YARN:

- ResourceManager
- NodeManager

ResourceManager

The **ResourceManager** daemon is a global master daemon that is responsible for managing the resources for the applications in the cluster. The ResourceManager daemon consists of the following two components:

- ApplicationsManager
- Scheduler

The ApplicationsManager performs the following operations:

- Accepts jobs from a client.
- Creates the first container on one of the worker nodes to host the **ApplicationMaster**. A container, in simple terms, is the memory resource on a single worker node in cluster.
- Restarts the container hosting ApplicationMaster on failure.

The scheduler is responsible for allocating the system resources to the various applications in the cluster and also performs the monitoring of each application.

Each application in YARN will have an ApplicationMaster. This is responsible for communicating with the scheduler and setting up and monitoring its resource containers.

NodeManager

The **NodeManager** daemon runs on the worker nodes and is responsible for monitoring the containers within the node and its system resources such as CPU, memory, and disk. It sends this monitoring information back to the ResourceManager daemon. Each worker node will have exactly one NodeManager daemon running.

Job submission in YARN

The following are the sequence of steps involved when a job is submitted to a YARN cluster:

1. When a job is submitted to the cluster, the client first receives an application ID from the ResourceManager.
2. Next, the client copies the job resources to a location in the HDFS.

3. The ResourceManager then starts the first container under the NodeManager's management to bring up the ApplicationMaster. For example, if a MapReduce job is submitted, the ResourceManager will bring up the MapReduce ApplicationMaster.

4. The ApplicationMaster, based on the job to be executed, requests resources from the ResourceManager.

5. Once the ResourceManager schedules a container with the requested resource, the ApplicationMaster contacts the NodeManager to start the container and execute the task. In case of a MapReduce job, that task would be a map or reduce task.

6. The client checks with the ApplicationMaster for status updates on the submitted job.

The following diagram shows the interactions of the client and the different daemons in a YARN environment:

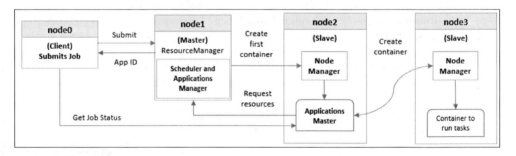

In a Hadoop cluster, the ResourceManager and NodeManager daemons can be monitored via specific URLs using a browser. The specific URLs are of the `http://<serveraddress>:port_number` type.

By default, the ports for these Hadoop daemons are:

The Hadoop daemon	Port
ResourceManager	8088
NodeManager	8042

The preceding mentioned ports can be configured in the `yarn-site.xml` file.

This was a short introduction to YARN, but it is important as a Hadoop administrator to know about YARN as this is soon going to be the way all Hadoop clusters will function.

Introducing Cloudera

Cloudera Inc. is a Palo Alto-based American enterprise software company that provides Apache Hadoop-based software, support and services, and training to data-driven enterprises. It is often referred to as the commercial Hadoop company.

Cloudera was founded by three top engineers from Google, Yahoo!, and Facebook—Christophe Bisciglia, Amr Awadallah, and Jeff Hammerbacher.

Cloudera is the market leader in Hadoop and is one of the major code contributors to the Apache Hadoop ecosystem. With the help of Hadoop, Cloudera helps businesses and organizations interact with their large datasets and derive great insights.

They have also built a full-fledged Apache Hadoop distribution called **Cloudera's Distribution Including** and a proprietary Hadoop cluster manager called **Cloudera Manager**, which helps users set up large clusters with extreme ease.

Introducing CDH

CDH or Cloudera's Distribution Including Apache Hadoop is an enterprise-level distribution including Apache Hadoop and several components of its ecosystem such as Apache Hive, Apache Avro, HBase, and many more. CDH is 100 percent open source. It is the most downloaded distribution in its space. As of writing this book, the current version of CDH is CDH 5.0.

Some of the important features of CDH are as follows:

- All components are thoroughly tested by Cloudera, to see that they work well with each other, making it a very stable distribution
- All enterprise needs such as security and high availability are built-in as part of the distribution
- The distribution is very well documented making it easy for anyone interested to get the services up and running quickly

Responsibilities of a Hadoop administrator

With the increase in the interest to derive insight on their big data, organizations are now planning and building their big data teams aggressively. To start working on their data, they need to have a good solid infrastructure. Once they have this setup, they need several controls and system policies in place to maintain, manage, and troubleshoot their cluster.

There is an ever-increasing demand for Hadoop Administrators in the market as their function (setting up and maintaining Hadoop clusters) is what makes analysis really possible.

The Hadoop administrator needs to be very good at system operations, networking, operating systems, and storage. They need to have a strong knowledge of computer hardware and their operations, in a complex network.

Apache Hadoop, mainly, runs on Linux. So having good Linux skills such as monitoring, troubleshooting, configuration, and security is a must.

Setting up nodes for clusters involves a lot of repetitive tasks and the Hadoop administrator should use quicker and efficient ways to bring up these servers using configuration management tools such as Puppet, Chef, and CFEngine. Apart from these tools, the administrator should also have good capacity planning skills to design and plan clusters.

There are several nodes in a cluster that would need duplication of data, for example, the fsimage file of the namenode daemon can be configured to write to two different disks on the same node or on a disk on a different node. An understanding of NFS mount points and how to set it up within a cluster is required. The administrator may also be asked to set up RAID for disks on specific nodes.

As all Hadoop services/daemons are built on Java, a basic knowledge of the JVM along with the ability to understand Java exceptions would be very useful. This helps administrators identify issues quickly.

The Hadoop administrator should possess the skills to benchmark the cluster to test performance under high traffic scenarios.

Clusters are prone to failures as they are up all the time and are processing large amounts of data regularly. To monitor the health of the cluster, the administrator should deploy monitoring tools such as Nagios and Ganglia and should configure alerts and monitors for critical nodes of the cluster to foresee issues before they occur.

Knowledge of a good scripting language such as Python, Ruby, or Shell would greatly help the function of an administrator. Often, administrators are asked to set up some kind of a scheduled file staging from an external source to HDFS. The scripting skills help them execute these requests by building scripts and automating them.

Above all, the Hadoop administrator should have a very good understanding of the Apache Hadoop architecture and its inner workings.

The following are some of the key Hadoop-related operations that the Hadoop administrator should know:

- Planning the cluster, deciding on the number of nodes based on the estimated amount of data the cluster is going to serve.
- Installing and upgrading Apache Hadoop on a cluster.
- Configuring and tuning Hadoop using the various configuration files available within Hadoop.
- An understanding of all the Hadoop daemons along with their roles and responsibilities in the cluster.
- The administrator should know how to read and interpret Hadoop logs.
- Adding and removing nodes in the cluster.
- Rebalancing nodes in the cluster.
- Employ security using an authentication and authorization system such as Kerberos.
- Almost all organizations follow the policy of backing up their data and it is the responsibility of the administrator to perform this activity. So, an administrator should be well versed with backups and recovery operations of servers.

Summary

In this chapter, we started out by exploring the history of Apache Hadoop and moved on to understanding its specific components. We also introduced ourselves to the new version of Apache Hadoop. We learned about Cloudera and its Apache Hadoop distribution called CDH and finally looked at some important roles and responsibilities of an Apache Hadoop administrator.

In the next chapter, we will get a more detailed understanding of Apache Hadoop's distributed filesystem, HDFS, and its programming model, MapReduce.

2
HDFS and MapReduce

We now have a basic understanding of the Apache Hadoop architecture and its inner workings. In this chapter, we will dive deeper into the two major components of Apache Hadoop—HDFS and MapReduce, and will cover the following topics:

- Essentials of Hadoop Distributed File System
- The read/write operational flow in HDFS
- Exploring HDFS commands
- Getting acquainted with MapReduce

Essentials of HDFS

HDFS is a distributed filesystem that has been designed to run on top of a cluster of industry standard hardware. The architecture of HDFS is such that there is no specific need for high-end hardware. HDFS is a highly fault-tolerant system and can handle failures of nodes in a cluster without loss of data. The primary goal behind the design of HDFS is to serve large data files efficiently. HDFS achieves this efficiency and high throughput in data transfer by enabling streaming access to the data in the filesystem.

The following are the important features of HDFS:

- **Fault tolerance**: Many computers working together as a cluster are bound to have hardware failures. Hardware failures such as disk failures, network connectivity issues, and RAM failures could disrupt processing and cause major downtime. This could lead to data loss as well slippage of critical SLAs. HDFS is designed to withstand such hardware failures by detecting faults and taking recovery actions as required.

The data in HDFS is split across the machines in the cluster as chunks of data called **blocks**. These blocks are replicated across multiple machines of the cluster for redundancy. So, even if a node/machine becomes completely unusable and shuts down, the processing can go on with the copy of the data present on the nodes where the data was replicated.

- **Streaming data**: Streaming access enables data to be transferred in the form of a steady and continuous stream. This means if data from a file in HDFS needs to be processed, HDFS starts sending the data as it reads the file and does not wait for the entire file to be read. The client who is consuming this data starts processing the data immediately, as it receives the stream from HDFS. This makes data processing really fast.

- **Large data store**: HDFS is used to store large volumes of data. HDFS functions best when the individual data files stored are large files, rather than having large number of small files. File sizes in most Hadoop clusters range from gigabytes to terabytes. The storage scales linearly as more nodes are added to the cluster.

- **Portable**: HDFS is a highly portable system. Since it is built on Java, any machine or operating system that can run Java should be able to run HDFS. Even at the hardware layer, HDFS is flexible and runs on most of the commonly available hardware platforms. Most production level clusters have been set up on commodity hardware.

- **Easy interface**: The HDFS command-line interface is very similar to any Linux/Unix system. The commands are similar in most cases. So, if one is comfortable with the performing basic file actions in Linux/Unix, using commands with HDFS should be very easy.

The following two daemons are responsible for operations on HDFS:

- Namenode
- Datanode

In *Chapter 1, Getting Started with Apache Hadoop*, we already covered the details on how the namenode and datanodes daemons work together to store files in the cluster. These daemons talk to each other via TCP/IP.

Configuring HDFS

All HDFS-related configuration is done by adding/updating the properties in the `hdfs-site.xml` file that is found in the `conf` folder under the Hadoop installation folder.

The following are the different properties that are part of the `hdfs-site.xml` file:

- `dfs.namenode.servicerpc-address`: This specifies the unique namenode RPC address in the cluster. Services/daemons such as the secondary namenode and datanode daemons use this address to connect to the namenode daemon whenever it needs to communicate. This property is shown in the following code snippet:

```
<property>
    <name>dfs.namenode.servicerpc-address</name>
    <value>node1.hcluster:8022</value>
</property>
```

- `dfs.namenode.http-address`: This specifies the URL that can be used to monitor the namenode daemon from a browser. This property is shown in the following code snippet:

```
<property>
    <name>dfs.namenode.http-address</name>
    <value>node1.hcluster:50070</value>
</property>
```

- `dfs.replication`: This specifies the replication factor for data block replication across the datanode daemons. The default is 3 as shown in the following code snippet:

```
<property>
    <name>dfs.replication</name>
    <value>3</value>
</property>
```

- `dfs.blocksize`: This specifies the block size. In the following example, the size is specified in bytes (134,217,728 bytes is 128 MB):

```
<property>
    <name>dfs.blocksize</name>
    <value>134217728</value>
</property>
```

- `fs.permissions.umask-mode`: This specifies the `umask` value that will be used when creating files and directories in HDFS. This property is shown in the following code snippet:

```
<property>
    <name>fs.permissions.umask-mode</name>
    <value>022</value>
</property>
```

The read/write operational flow in HDFS

To get a better understanding of HDFS, we need to understand the flow of operations for the following two scenarios:

- A file is written to HDFS
- A file is read from HDFS

HDFS uses a single-write, multiple-read model, where the files are written once and read several times. The data cannot be altered once written. However, data can be appended to the file by reopening it. All files in the HDFS are saved as data blocks.

Writing files in HDFS

The following sequence of steps occur when a client tries to write a file to HDFS:

1. The client informs the namenode daemon that it wants to write a file. The namenode daemon checks to see whether the file already exists.

2. If it exists, an appropriate message is sent back to the client. If it does not exist, the namenode daemon makes a metadata entry for the new file.

3. The file to be written is split into data packets at the client end and a data queue is built. The packets in the queue are then streamed to the datanodes in the cluster.

4. The list of datanodes is given by the namenode daemon, which is prepared based on the data replication factor configured. A pipeline is built to perform the writes to all datanodes provided by the namenode daemon.

5. The first packet from the data queue is then transferred to the first datanode daemon. The block is stored on the first datanode daemon and is then copied to the next datanode daemon in the pipeline. This process goes on till the packet is written to the last datanode daemon in the pipeline.

6. The sequence is repeated for all the packets in the data queue. For every packet written on the datanode daemon, a corresponding acknowledgement is sent back to the client.

7. If a packet fails to write onto one of the datanodes, the datanode daemon is removed from the pipeline and the remainder of the packets is written to the good datanodes. The namenode daemon notices the under-replication of the block and arranges for another datanode daemon where the block could be replicated.

8. After all the packets are written, the client performs a close action, indicating that the packets in the data queue have been completely transferred.

9. The client informs the namenode daemon that the write operation is now complete.

The following diagram shows the data block replication process across the datanodes during a write operation in HDFS:

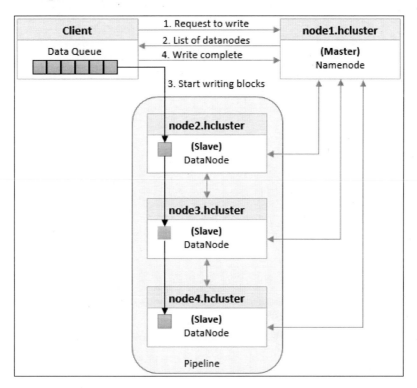

Reading files in HDFS

The following steps occur when a client tries to read a file in HDFS:

1. The client contacts the namenode daemon to get the location of the data blocks of the file it wants to read.

2. The namenode daemon returns the list of addresses of the datanodes for the data blocks.

3. For any read operation, HDFS tries to return the node with the data block that is closest to the client. Here, closest refers to network proximity between the datanode daemon and the client.

4. Once the client has the list, it connects the closest datanode daemon and starts reading the data block using a stream.

5. After the block is read completely, the connection to datanode is terminated and the datanode daemon that hosts the next block in the sequence is identified and the data block is streamed. This goes on until the last data block for that file is read.

The following diagram shows the read operation of a file in HDFS:

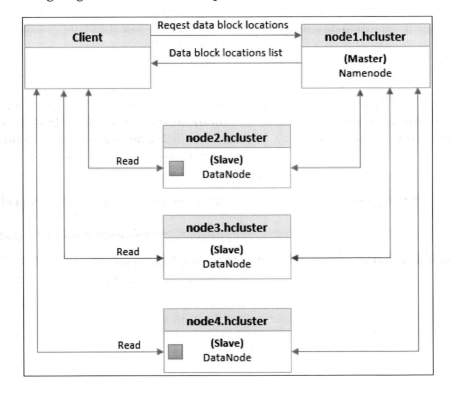

Understanding the namenode UI

Hadoop provides web interfaces for each of its services. The namenode UI or the namenode web interface is used to monitor the status of the namenode and can be accessed using the following URL:

```
http://<namenode-server>:50070/
```

The namenode UI has the following sections:

- **Overview**: The general information section provides basic information of the namenode with options to browse the filesystem and the namenode logs.

    The following is the screenshot of the **Overview** section of the namenode UI:

Overview 'node1.hcluster:8020' (active)	
Started:	Mon May 05 01:16:24 MDT 2014
Version:	2.3.0-cdh5.0.0, r8e266e052e423af592671e2dfe09d54c03f6a0e8
Compiled:	2014-03-28T04:30Z by jenkins from (no branch)
Cluster ID:	cluster42
Block Pool ID:	BP-2000146897-10.1.3.101-1399252482038

    The **Cluster ID** parameter displays the identification number of the cluster. This number is same across all the nodes within the cluster.

    A **block pool** is a set of blocks that belong to a single namespace. The **Block Pool Id** parameter is used to segregate the block pools in case there are multiple namespaces configured when using HDFS federation. In HDFS federation, multiple namenodes are configured to scale the name service horizontally. These namenodes are configured to share datanodes amongst themselves. We will be exploring HDFS federation in detail a bit later.

- **Summary**: The following is the screenshot of the cluster's summary section from the namenode web interface:

Summary

Security is off.

Safemode is off.

29 files and directories, 14 blocks = 43 total filesystem object(s).

Heap Memory used 243.71 MB of 990.75 MB Heap Memory. Max Heap Memory is 990.75 MB.

Non Heap Memory used 46.11 MB of 46.44 MB Commited Non Heap Memory. Max Non Heap Memory is 130 MB.

Configured Capacity:	161.69 GB
DFS Used:	418.23 MB
Non DFS Used:	27.86 GB
DFS Remaining:	133.43 GB
DFS Used%:	0.25%
DFS Remaining%:	82.52%
Block Pool Used:	418.23 MB
Block Pool Used%:	0.25%
DataNodes usages% (Min/Median/Max/stdDev):	0.16% / 0.29% / 0.34% / 0.07%
Live Nodes	4 (Decommissioned: 0)
Dead Nodes	0 (Decommissioned: 0)
Decommissioning Nodes	0
Number of Under-Replicated Blocks	0

Under the **Summary** section, the first parameter is related to the security configuration of the cluster. If Kerberos (the authorization and authentication system used in Hadoop) is configured, the parameter will show as **Security is on**. If Kerberos is not configured, the parameter will show as **Security is off**.

The next parameter displays information related to files and blocks in the cluster. Along with this information, the heap and non-heap memory utilization is also displayed. The other parameters displayed in the **Summary** section are as follows:

- ° **Configured Capacity**: This displays the total capacity (storage space) of HDFS.

- ° **DFS Used**: This displays the total space used in HDFS.

- ° **Non DFS Used**: This displays the amount of space used by other files that are not part of HDFS. This is the space used by the operating system and other files.

- ° **DFS Remaining**: This displays the total space remaining in HDFS.

- ° **DFS Used%**: This displays the total HDFS space utilization shown as percentage.

- ° **DFS Remaining%**: This displays the total HDFS space remaining shown as percentage.

- ° **Block Pool Used**: This displays the total space utilized by the current namespace.

- ° **Block Pool Used%**: This displays the total space utilized by the current namespace shown as percentage. As you can see in the preceding screenshot, in this case, the value matches that of the **DFS Used%** parameter. This is because there is only one namespace (one namenode) and HDFS is not federated.

- ° **DataNodes usages% (Min, Median, Max, stdDev)**: This displays the usages across all datanodes in the cluster. This helps administrators identify unbalanced nodes, which may occur when data is not uniformly placed across the datanodes. Administrators have the option to rebalance the datanodes using a balancer.

- ° **Live Nodes**: This link displays all the datanodes in the cluster as shown in the following screenshot:

Datanode Information

In operation

Node	Last contact	Admin State	Capacity	Used	Non DFS Used	Remaining	Blocks	Block pool used	Failed Volumes	Version
node1.hcluster (10.1.3.101:50010)	2	In Service	40.42 GB	139.4 MB	13.74 GB	26.54 GB	14	139.4 MB (0.34%)	0	2.3.0-cdh5.0.0
node4.hcluster (10.1.3.104:50010)	2	In Service	40.42 GB	68.28 MB	5.87 GB	34.48 GB	7	68.28 MB (0.16%)	0	2.3.0-cdh5.0.0
node3.hcluster (10.1.3.103:50010)	0	In Service	40.42 GB	91.45 MB	4.18 GB	36.16 GB	9	91.45 MB (0.22%)	0	2.3.0-cdh5.0.0
node2.hcluster (10.1.3.102:50010)	0	In Service	40.42 GB	119.09 MB	4.06 GB	36.24 GB	12	119.09 MB (0.29%)	0	2.3.0-cdh5.0.0

Decomissioning

Node	Last contact	Under replicated blocks	Blocks with no live replicas	Under Replicated Blocks In files under construction

Hadoop, 2014

- ° **Dead Nodes**: This link displays all the datanodes that are currently in a dead state in the cluster. A **dead state** for a datanode daemon is when the datanode daemon is not running or has not sent a heartbeat message to the namenode daemon. Datanodes are unable to send heartbeats if there exists a network connection issue between the machines that host the datanode and namenode daemons. Excessive swapping on the datanode machine causes the machine to become unresponsive, which also prevents the datanode daemon from sending heartbeats.

- ° **Decommissioning Nodes**: This link lists all the datanodes that are being decommissioned.

- ° **Number of Under-Replicated Blocks**: This represents the number of blocks that have not replicated as per the replication factor configured in the `hdfs-site.xml` file.

- **Namenode Journal Status**: The journal status provides location information of the `fsimage` file and the state of the `edits` logfile. The following screenshot shows the **NameNode Journal Status** section:

NameNode Journal Status

Current transaction ID: 47033

Journal Manager	State
FileJournalManager(root=/dfs/nn)	EditLogFileOutputStream(/dfs/nn/current/edits_inprogress_0000000000000046985)

- **NameNode Storage**: The namenode storage table provides the location of the `fsimage` file along with the type of the location. In this case, it is `IMAGE_AND_EDITS`, which means the same location is used to store the `fsimage` file as well as the `edits` logfile. The other types of locations are `IMAGE`, which stores only the `fsimage` file and `EDITS`, which stores only the `edits` logfile. The following screenshot shows the **NameNode Storage** information:

NameNode Storage

Storage Directory	Type	State
/dfs/nn	IMAGE_AND_EDITS	Active

Understanding the secondary namenode UI

The secondary namenode is a checkpoint service for the namenode daemon that performs periodic merging of the `edits` log and the `fsimage` file. The secondary namenode UI can be accessed using the following URL:

```
http://<secondary-namenode-server>:50090/
```

The following screenshot shows the secondary namenode UI:

```
SecondaryNameNode

Version:    2.3.0-cdh5.0.0, 8e266e052e423af592871e2dfe09d54c03f6a0e8
Compiled:   2014-03-28T04:30Z by jenkins from (no branch)


SecondaryNameNode Status
Name Node Address    : node1.hcluster/10.1.3.101:8022
Start Time           : Mon May 05 01:16:22 MDT 2014
Last Checkpoint Time : Sat May 10 11:18:50 MDT 2014
Checkpoint Period    : 3600 seconds
Checkpoint Size      : 976.56 KB (= 1000000 bytes)
Checkpoint Dirs      : [file:///dfs/snn]
Checkpoint Edits Dirs: [file:///dfs/snn]


Logs

Hadoop, 2014.
```

Just like the namenode UI, the secondary namenode UI also displays the Hadoop version. All checkpoint related information is available in this UI, which are given as follows:

- **Name Node Address**: This is the RPC address of the primary namenode daemon. Secondary namenode uses this address to connect to primary namenode.

- **Start Time**: This is the start timestamp of the secondary namenode service.

- **Last Checkpoint Time**: This the timestamp of the last checkpoint action performed by the secondary namenode daemon.

- **Checkpoint Period**: This property defines the schedule to perform the checkpoint. In the preceding screenshot, the value is **3,600 seconds**. This means that every 3,600 seconds (1 hour), the secondary namenode daemon will perform the checkpoint operation.

- **Checkpoint Size**: If the `edits` logfile reaches this checkpoint size, the secondary namenode daemon will perform the checkpoint even if the check point period has not elapsed.

- **Checkpoint Dirs**: This is the location of the `fsimage` file stored by the secondary namenode daemon.

- **Checkpoint Edit Dirs**: This is the location of the `edits` logfiles stored by the secondary namenode daemon.

Exploring HDFS commands

To perform filesystem related tasks, the commands begin with `hdfs dfs`. The filesystem commands have been designed to behave similarly to the corresponding Unix/Linux filesystem commands.

What is a URI? **URI** stands for **Uniform Resource Identifier**. In the commands that are listed as follows, you will observe the use of URI for file locations. The URI syntax to access a file in HDFS is `hdfs://namenodehost/parent/child/<file>`.

Commonly used HDFS commands

The following are some of the most commonly used HDFS commands:

- `ls`: This command lists files in HDFS.

  The syntax of the `ls` command is `hdfs dfs -ls <args>`. The following is the screenshot showing an example of the `ls` command:

```
[root@node1 data]# hdfs dfs -ls /user/root/source/
Found 12 items
-rw-r--r--   3 root root   10576161 2014-05-11 14:18 /user/root/source/file1.txt
-rw-r--r--   3 root root   10570494 2014-05-11 14:18 /user/root/source/file10.txt
-rw-r--r--   3 root root   10553286 2014-05-11 14:18 /user/root/source/file11.txt
-rw-r--r--   3 root root   10580789 2014-05-11 14:18 /user/root/source/file12.txt
-rw-r--r--   3 root root   10571366 2014-05-11 14:18 /user/root/source/file2.txt
-rw-r--r--   3 root root   10561045 2014-05-11 14:18 /user/root/source/file3.txt
-rw-r--r--   3 root root   10553346 2014-05-11 14:18 /user/root/source/file4.txt
-rw-r--r--   3 root root   10555458 2014-05-11 14:18 /user/root/source/file5.txt
-rw-r--r--   3 root root   10562324 2014-05-11 14:18 /user/root/source/file6.txt
-rw-r--r--   3 root root   10556108 2014-05-11 14:18 /user/root/source/file7.txt
-rw-r--r--   3 root root   10548089 2014-05-11 14:18 /user/root/source/file8.txt
-rw-r--r--   3 root root   10587287 2014-05-11 14:18 /user/root/source/file9.txt
[root@node1 data]#
```

- `cat`: This command displays the contents of file/files in the terminal.

  The syntax of the `cat` command is `hdfs dfs -cat URI [URI ...]`. The following is a sample output of the `cat` command:

```
[root@node1 data]# hdfs dfs -cat /user/root/source/file2.txt
[[List of artificial intelligence projects]]

===Planning===

===Other===

==Multipurpose projects==

===Software libraries===
```

- `copyFromLocal`: This command copies a file/files from the local filesystem to HDFS.

  The syntax of the `copyFromLocal` command is `hdfs dfs -copyFromLocal <localsrc> URI`. The following is the screenshot showing an example of the `copyFromLocal` command:

```
[root@node1 data]# hdfs dfs -copyFromLocal file1.txt /user/root/files
[root@node1 data]# hdfs dfs -ls /user/root/files
Found 1 items
-rw-r--r--   3 root root   10576161 2014-05-11 15:31 /user/root/files/file1.txt
[root@node1 data]#
```

- `copyToLocal`: This command copies a file/files from HDFS to the local filesystem.

  The syntax of the `copyToLocal` command is `hdfs dfs -copyToLocal URI <localdst>`. The following is the screenshot showing an example of the `copyToLocal` command:

```
[root@node1 data]# hdfs dfs -copyToLocal /user/root/files/file1.txt file_from_hdfs.txt
[root@node1 data]# ls -ltr file_from_hdfs.txt
-rw-r--r-- 1 root root 10576161 May 11 15:35 file_from_hdfs.txt
[root@node1 data]#
```

- cp: This command copies files within HDFS.

  The syntax of the cp command is hdfs dfs -cp URI [URI ...] <dest>.
  The following is the screenshot showing an example of the cp command:

```
[root@node1 data]# hdfs dfs -cp source/file1.txt dest/
[root@node1 data]# hdfs dfs -ls dest/
Found 1 items
-rw-r--r--   3 root root   10576161 2014-05-11 15:57 dest/file1.txt
[root@node1 data]#
```

- mkdir: This command creates a directory in HDFS.

  The syntax of the mkdir command is hdfs dfs -mkdir <paths>.
  The following is the screenshot showing an example of the mkdir command:

```
[root@node1 data]# hdfs dfs -mkdir /user/root/target
[root@node1 data]# hdfs dfs -ls /user/root
Found 3 items
drwxr-xr-x   - root root          0 2014-05-10 13:01 /user/root/destination
drwxr-xr-x   - root root          0 2014-05-10 12:46 /user/root/source
drwxr-xr-x   - root root          0 2014-05-10 13:03 /user/root/target
[root@node1 data]#
```

- mv: This command moves files within HDFS.

  The syntax of the mv command is hdfs dfs -mv URI [URI ...] <dest>.
  The following is the screenshot showing an example of the mv command:

```
[root@node1 data]# hdfs dfs -mv source/file2.txt dest/file2.txt
[root@node1 data]# hdfs dfs -ls dest/
Found 2 items
-rw-r--r--   3 root root   10576161 2014-05-11 15:57 dest/file1.txt
-rw-r--r--   3 root root   10571366 2014-05-11 14:18 dest/file2.txt
[root@node1 data]#
```

- rm: This command deletes files from HDFS.

  The syntax of the rm command is hdfs dfs -rm URI [URI ...].
  The following is the screenshot showing an example of the rm command:

```
[root@node1 data]# hdfs dfs -rm dest/*.txt
14/05/11 16:01:31 INFO fs.TrashPolicyDefault: Namenode trash configuration: Deletion interval = 1440 minutes, Emptier interval = 0 minutes.
Moved: 'hdfs://node1.hcluster:8020/user/root/dest/file1.txt' to trash at: hdfs://node1.hcluster:8020/user/root/.Trash/Current
14/05/11 16:01:31 INFO fs.TrashPolicyDefault: Namenode trash configuration: Deletion interval = 1440 minutes, Emptier interval = 0 minutes.
Moved: 'hdfs://node1.hcluster:8020/user/root/dest/file2.txt' to trash at: hdfs://node1.hcluster:8020/user/root/.Trash/Current
[root@node1 data]#
```

- `rm -r`: This command deletes a directory from the HDFS.

  The syntax of the `rm -r` command is `hdfs dfs -rm -r URI [URI ...]`.
  The following is the screenshot showing an example of the `rm -r` command:

```
[root@node1 data]# hdfs dfs -ls /user/root/
Found 4 items
drwx------   - root root          0 2014-05-10 13:27 /user/root/.Trash
drwxr-xr-x   - root root          0 2014-05-10 13:07 /user/root/destination
drwxr-xr-x   - root root          0 2014-05-10 12:46 /user/root/source
drwxr-xr-x   - root root          0 2014-05-10 13:27 /user/root/target
[root@node1 data]# hdfs dfs -rm -r /user/root/target
14/05/10 13:29:33 INFO fs.TrashPolicyDefault: Namenode trash configuration: Deletion interval = 1440 minutes, Emptier interval = 0 minutes.
Moved: 'hdfs://node1.hcluster:8020/user/root/target' to trash at: hdfs://node1.hcluster:8020/user/root/.Trash/Current
[root@node1 data]#
```

- `setrep`: This command sets the replication factor for a file in HDFS.

  The syntax of the `setrep` command is `hdfs dfs -setrep [-R] <path>`.
  The following is the screenshot showing an example of the `setrep` command:

```
[root@node1 data]# hdfs dfs -setrep -w 4 /user/root/destination/enwiki-20130102-pages-articles.xml-001.txt
Replication 4 set: /user/root/destination/enwiki-20130102-pages-articles.xml-001.txt
Waiting for /user/root/destination/enwiki-20130102-pages-articles.xml-001.txt .... done
```

- `tail`: This command displays the trailing kilobyte of the contents of a file in HDFS.

  The syntax of the `tail` command is `hdfs dfs -tail [-f] URI`.
  The following is the screenshot showing an example of the `tail` command:

```
[root@node1 data]# hdfs dfs -tail /user/root/destination/enwiki-20130102-pages-articles.xml-001.txt
o a colour TV when run in its low or medium resolution (525/625 line 60/50 Hz interlace, even on RGB
ptionally crisp and clear, monitor). These models were known as the 520STM (or 520STM). Later F and

=== STE ===

As originally released in the 520STE/1040STE:

== Models ==
```

Commands to administer HDFS

Hadoop provides several commands to administer HDFS. The following are two of the commonly used administration commands in HDFS:

- `balancer`: In a cluster, new datanodes can be added. The addition of new datanodes provides more storage space for the cluster. However, when a new datanode is added, the datanode does not have any files. Due to the addition of the new datanode, data blocks across all the datanodes are in a state of imbalance, that is, they are not evenly spread across the datanodes. The administrator can use the `balancer` command to balance the cluster. The balancer can be invoked using this command.

The syntax of the `balancer` command is `hdfs balancer -threshold <threshold>`. Here, `threshold` is the balancing threshold expressed in percentage. The threshold is specified as a float value that ranges from 0 to 100. The default threshold values is 10. The balancer tries to distribute blocks to the underutilized datanodes. For example, if the average utilization of all the datanodes in the cluster is 50 percent, the balancer, by default, will try to pick up blocks from nodes that have a utilization of above 60 percent (50 percent + 10 percent) and move them to nodes that have a utilization of below 40 percent (50 percent - 10 percent).

- `dfsadmin`: The `dfsadmin` command is used to run administrative commands on HDFS.

  The syntax of the `dfsadmin` command is `hadoop dfsadmin <options>`. Let's understand a few of the important command options and the actions they perform:

  ◦ `[-report]`: This generates a report of the basic filesystem information and statistics.

  ◦ `[-safemode <enter | leave | get | wait>]`: This safe mode is a namenode state in which it does not accept changes to the namespace (read-only) and does not replicate or delete blocks.

  ◦ `[-saveNamespace]`: This saves the current state of the namespace to a storage directory and resets the `edits` log.

  ◦ `[-rollEdits]`: This forces a rollover of the `edits` log, that is, it saves the state of the current `edits` log and creates a fresh `edits` log for new transactions.

  ◦ `[-restoreFailedStorage true|false|check]`: This enables to set/unset or check to attempt to restore failed storage replicas.

  ◦ `[-refreshNodes]`: This updates the namenode daemon with the set of datanodes allowed to connect to the namenode daemon.

  ◦ `[-setQuota <quota> <dirname>...<dirname>]`: This sets the quota (the number of items) for the directory/directories.

  ◦ `[-clrQuota <dirname>...<dirname>]`: This clears the set quota for the directory/directories.

  ◦ `[-setSpaceQuota <quota> <dirname>...<dirname>]`: This sets the disk space quota for the directory/directories.

  ◦ `[-clrSpaceQuota <dirname>...<dirname>]`: This clears the disk space quota for the directory/directories.

  ◦ `[-refreshserviceacl]`: This refreshes the service-level authorization policy file. We will be learning more about authorization later.

- ° `[-printTopology]`: This prints the tree of the racks and their nodes as reported by the namenode daemon.

- ° `[-refreshNamenodes datanodehost:port]`: This reloads the configuration files for a datanode daemon, stops serving the removed block pools, and starts serving new block pools. A block pool is a set of blocks that belong to a single namespace. We will be looking into this concept a bit later.

- ° `[-deleteBlockPool datanodehost:port blockpoolId [force]]`: This deletes a block pool of a datanode daemon.

- ° `[-setBalancerBandwidth <bandwidth>]`: This sets the bandwidth limit to be used by the balancer. The bandwidth is the value in bytes per second that the balancer should use for data blocks movement.

- ° `[-fetchImage <local directory>]`: This gets the latest `fsimage` file from namenode and saves it to the specified local directory.

- ° `[-help [cmd]]`: This displays help for the given command or all commands if a command is not specified.

Getting acquainted with MapReduce

Now you have a solid knowledge base in HDFS, it is now time to dive into the processing module of Hadoop known as MapReduce. Once we have the data in the cluster, we need a programming model to perform advanced operations on it. This is done using Hadoop's MapReduce.

The MapReduce programming model concept has been in existence for quite some time now. This model was designed to process large volumes of data in parallel. Google implemented a version of MapReduce in house to process their data stored on GFS. Later, Google released a paper explaining their implementation. Hadoop's MapReduce implementation is based on this paper.

MapReduce in Hadoop is a Java-based distributed programming framework that leverages the features of HDFS to execute high performance batch processing of the data stored in HDFS.

The processing can be divided into major functions, which are:

- Map
- Reduce

Since the primary focus of this book is on the administrative aspects of Hadoop, we will focus on the MapReduce architecture and how it works together with HDFS to process large volumes of data.

Understanding the map phase

In a MapReduce application, all the data read in the map function is read in the form of **key** and **value** pairs. The processed output of the map function is also in the form of key and value pairs. The processing of data as key and value pairs works well in a distributed computing environment.

Let's understand how MapReduce works with the help of an example. The word counting program is known as the **Hello, World** program for MapReduce. The program counts the number of words in an input set of text files.

For this example, let's consider a file with the following line in it:

```
She sells sea shells on the sea shore where she also sells
cookies.
```

So, if the preceding text is provided as an input to the word count program, the expected output would be as follows:

```
she, 2
sells,2
sea, 2
shells, 1
on, 1
the, 1
shore, 1
where, 1
also, 1
cookies, 1
```

The three major components of a MapReduce program are:

- Driver
- Mapper
- Reducer

The driver component of a MapReduce program is responsible for setting up the job configurations and submitting it to the Hadoop cluster. This part of the program runs on the client computer.

The driver component of the word count program would take two parameters to submit the job to the Hadoop cluster:

- The location of the input files
- The location of the output file

Once the job is submitted to the cluster, the mapper reads every line in the file as <key, value> pairs. So, if we consider a file with the line mentioned earlier, the key will be the offset of the line and the value will be the entire sentence.

The mapper reads the line as follows:

```
<0000, She sells sea shells on the sea shore where she also sells
cookies>
```

Once read, the mapper logic would emit the <key, value> pairs for each word in the sentence as follows:

```
<she, 1>
<sells, 1>
<sea, 1>
<shells, 1>
<on, 1>
<the, 1>
<sea, 1>
<shore, 1>
<where, 1>
<she, 1>
<also, 1>
<sells, 1>
<cookies, 1>
```

The mapping function has emitted each word in the sentence as a key and constant number 1 as the value for each key.

Understanding the reduce phase

The reduce function reads the intermediate <key, value> pairs emitted by the mapper and produces the final result.

These results are then taken as input by the reducer in a sorted order of the keys. The reducer logic would then work on each key group; in this case, it would sum up the values for each key and would produce the final result as follows:

```
she, 2
sells,2
sea, 2
shells, 1
on, 1
the, 1
shore, 1
where, 1
also, 1
cookies, 1
```

The following is a functional representation of the map and reduce functions:

Function	Input	Output
map	<k1, v1>	list(k2, v2)
reduce	<k2, list(v2)>	list(<k3, v3>)

The following diagram shows the flow of a MapReduce job starting from an input file right up to the generation of an output file:

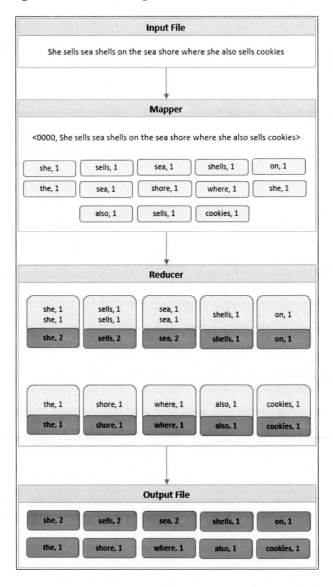

In the preceding diagram, you see a very simple flow of MapReduce. However, in real production scenarios, there are multiple mappers and reducers.

When there are multiple mappers and reducers involved, there is a phase between the mapper and reducer known as the **shuffle and sort** phase. In this phase, all the keys are sorted and sent to the reducers. Each reducer works on the set of keys and values provided as input and generates their own output file as shown in the following diagram:

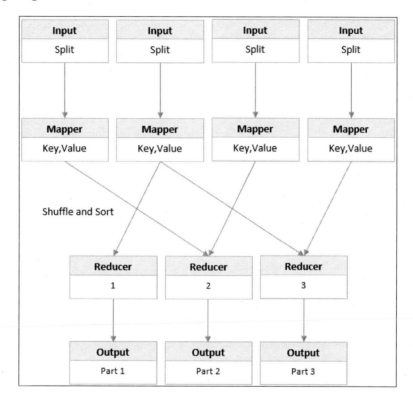

Learning all about the MapReduce job flow

There are several operations and services involved in the submission and execution of a MapReduce job in a Hadoop cluster.

The two main services that are responsible for job execution are:

- Jobtracker
- Tasktracker

When a client initiates a job submission to the cluster, a new job ID is created by the jobtracker and returned to the client. After getting the ID, the job resources along with the information on the input splits of the data are then copied to HDFS so that all the services in the cluster can access it. The client then polls the jobtracker every second to check the job's completion status.

The jobtracker then takes over and initializes the job in the cluster by accessing the job resources in HDFS. The jobtracker retrieves the input splits information and then decides the tasks that it needs to assign to tasktrackers. The job tracker creates a map task for each of the input splits and then assigns the map tasks to the tasktrackers. The tasktrackers are also responsible for running the reduce tasks on completion of the map tasks. The jobtracker tries to assign map tasks to tasktrackers on nodes that are in close proximity to the data. This greatly improves performance by limiting the data transferred across the network (data locality).

The tasktracker is the actual service that runs a task. Tasktrackers are running all the time and are waiting for tasks to be assigned to them by the jobtracker. Tasktrackers are configured to run a specific number of map and reduce tasks. These are called **slots**.

The tasktracker sends a periodic heartbeat to the jobtracker to inform it that it is alive along with the number of map and reduce slots it has available. The jobtracker assigns tasks as a return value for the heartbeat. Once the task is assigned, the tasktracker copies the client program (usually a java compiled set of classes, referred to as a **jar**) to its local space from HDFS. All the intermediate data generated by the map task is stored locally on the node where the tasktracker runs.

After all the map and reduce tasks are completed, the jobtracker receives a notification of completion. The jobtracker marks the job as successful. The client that polls for the status of the job prints the completion notification on the client console.

Configuring MapReduce

All MapReduce-related configuration is done by adding/updating the properties in the `mapred-site.xml` file. The following is an example of a `mapred-site.xml` file:

```
<?xml version="1.0" encoding="UTF-8"?>
<configuration>
  <property>
    <name>mapred.job.tracker</name>
    <value>node1.hcluster:8021</value>
  </property>
  <property>
    <name>mapred.job.tracker.http.address</name>
    <value>0.0.0.0:50030</value>
  </property>
```

```
<property>
  <name>mapreduce.job.counters.max</name>
  <value>120</value>
</property>
<property>
  <name>mapred.output.compress</name>
  <value>false</value>
</property>
<property>
  <name>mapred.output.compression.type</name>
  <value>BLOCK</value>
</property>
<property>
  <name>mapred.output.compression.codec</name>
  <value>org.apache.hadoop.io.compress.DefaultCodec</value>
</property>
<property>
  <name>mapred.map.output.compression.codec</name>
  <value>org.apache.hadoop.io.compress.SnappyCodec</value>
</property>
<property>
  <name>mapred.compress.map.output</name>
  <value>true</value>
</property>
<property>
  <name>io.sort.mb</name>
  <value>50</value>
</property>
<property>
  <name>io.sort.factor</name>
  <value>64</value>
</property>
<property>
  <name>mapred.reduce.parallel.copies</name>
  <value>10</value>
</property>
<property>
  <name>mapred.submit.replication</name>
  <value>2</value>
</property>
<property>
  <name>mapred.reduce.tasks</name>
  <value>4</value>
</property>
<property>
  <name>mapred.userlog.retain.hours</name>
  <value>24</value>
</property>
<property>
  <name>mapred.child.java.opts</name>
```

```
    <value> -Xmx112889935</value>
  </property>
  <property>
    <name>mapred.job.reuse.jvm.num.tasks</name>
    <value>1</value>
  </property>
  <property>
    <name>mapred.map.tasks.speculative.execution</name>
    <value>false</value>
  </property>
  <property>
    <name>mapred.reduce.tasks.speculative.execution</name>
    <value>false</value>
  </property>
  <property>
    <name>mapred.reduce.slowstart.completed.maps</name>
    <value>0.8</value>
  </property>
</configuration>
```

Let's discuss each property in detail:

- `mapred.job.tracker`: This property defines the host and port on which the jobtracker runs. All communication with the jobtracker is done over the host and port.

- `mapred.job.tracker.http.address`: This property defines the web address of the jobtracker. This web location helps in the monitoring of jobs submitted to the cluster.

- `mapreduce.job.counters.max`: Internally, Hadoop maintains several counters, for example, `JobCounter` and `TaskCounter` to count the job and task-related information during their process. However, it is also possible for developers to define their own counters. This liberty could cause issues if the number of counters is not controlled, as the jobtracker maintains these counters globally. This property helps in limiting the number of counters that can be generated.

- `mapred.output.compress`: This is a Boolean property, and if set to `true`, it will compress the job's output file.

- `mapred.output.compression.type`: This property defines the type of compression that can be set. The options are NONE, RECORD, or BLOCK.

- `mapred.output.compression.codec`: This property defines the codec to be used for compression of the job's output file.

- `mapred.map.output.compression.codec`: This property defines the codec that should be used to compress the map output files.

- `mapred.compress.map.output`: This property, if set to `true`, can compress the map output files before it is sent across the network.

- `io.sort.mb`: This property defines the memory set to perform the in-memory sorting and is useful when tuning to reduce the number of spilled records.

- `io.sort.factor`: When output data generated from a map task is small enough to fit into a tasktracker's memory, it is retained there and all operations are done in-memory. However, if the data is larger than the tasktracker's memory, it is spilled (written) to the disk. This property defines the number of open file handles that will be used when sorting files.

- `mapred.reduce.parallel.copies`: This property defines the number of parallel transfers done by reduce during the shuffle phase.

- `mapred.submit.replication`: This property defines the replication factor for the job-related resources that are copied to HDFS at the initiation of a job run.

- `mapred.reduce.tasks`: This property defines the number of reduce tasks for a single job.

- `mapred.userlog.retain.hours`: This property defines the retention period of the user logs after the job completion.

- `mapred.child.java.opts`: This property defines the parameters that are passed to the tasktracker's child processes.

- `mapred.job.reuse.jvm.num.tasks`: The tasktracker creates a JVM for each task. This property helps to alter this behavior to run more than one task per JVM.

- `mapred.map.tasks.speculative.execution`: Speculative execution is the ability of the jobtracker to identify slow running tasks and start another instance of the same task in parallel. The results of the task that finishes first will be considered and the incomplete task is discarded. This helps in situations when nodes that are running tasks face some kind of performance problems. If this property is set to `true`, two instances of the same map task could run in parallel.

- `mapred.reduce.tasks.speculative.execution`: If this property is set to `true`, multiple instances of the same reduce task can run in parallel.

- `mapred.reduce.slowstart.completed.maps`: This property defines the percentage value of how much a map task should complete before the reducers are scheduled for their tasks.

Understanding the jobtracker UI

The jobtracker user interface provides useful information related to the jobs executed on the cluster. The jobtracker status can be monitored via the following jobtracker URL:

```
http://<serveraddress>:50030/
```

The UI provides complete information of the status of the jobtracker along with the progress information of the task. The jobtracker page is divided into the following sections:

- **General Information**: The general information section displays some basic information of the jobtracker such as the current status, the timestamp of when the service was started, the compilation information, and a unique identifier for the service.

    The following screenshot shows the **General Information** section of the jobtracker web interface:

    node1 Hadoop Map/Reduce Administration

    State: RUNNING
    Started: Tue Oct 22 16:56:57 MDT 2013
    Version: 2.0.0-mr1-cdh4.4.0, Unknown
    Compiled: Tue Sep 3 19:45:53 PDT 2013 by jenkins from Unknown
    Identifier: 201310221656

- **Cluster Summary**: This section displays information about the tasks and nodes available in the cluster. Information such as the current running map and reduce tasks and number of nodes in the cluster are self-explanatory. Every tasktracker in the cluster has a configured number of map and reduce slots. The occupied map slots shows the number of map slots currently in use out of the total number of slots available in the cluster. Similarly, the occupied reduce slots show the number of reduce slots currently in use out the total available. The map task capacity and reduce task capacity is the value that represents the maximum number of map tasks and reduce tasks that can be run on the cluster. The average tasks per node shows the average number of map or reduces tasks that run on the cluster.

    If a node is not performing correctly, the jobtracker can blacklist the node so that no new tasks are assigned to it. The **Blacklisted Nodes** column in the **Cluster Summary** table shows the number of blacklisted nodes in the cluster. The excluded nodes show the number of decommissioned nodes in the cluster.

The following screenshot shows the **Cluster Summary** section of the jobtracker web interface:

Cluster Summary (Heap Size is 81.06 MB/105.94 MB)						
Running Map Tasks	Running Reduce Tasks	Total Submissions	Nodes	Occupied Map Slots	Occupied Reduce Slots	Reserved Map Slots
15	4	12	4	15	4	0

Reserved Reduce Slots	Map Task Capacity	Reduce Task Capacity	Avg. Tasks/Node	Blacklisted Nodes	Excluded Nodes
0	16	8	6.00	0	0

- **Scheduling Information**: This section shows the job scheduler information for the cluster. Here, the default job scheduler is a hyperlink that can be clicked to see the information of the jobs that are currently in queue. The default scheduler maintains a queue of all the jobs submitted and completes jobs sequentially. There are other types of the schedulers too that can be configured to run jobs in Hadoop, such as fair scheduler and capacity scheduler.

The following screenshot shows the **Scheduling Information** section of the jobtracker web interface:

Scheduling Information		
Queue Name	State	Scheduling Information
default	running	N/A

- **Running Jobs**: This section shows the details of the current running jobs in the cluster. This is very useful to monitor the status of the jobs. The **Jobid** column lists all the job IDs and each of them are hyperlinks. Clicking on one will bring up more details of the job. Some other basic job-related information such as the job priority, the user who submitted the job, and the name of the job are also displayed. The progress of the cumulative map and reduce tasks are also shown as percentages. Total map tasks, completed map tasks, total reduce tasks, and completed reduce task are also displayed.

The following screenshot shows the **Running Jobs** section of the jobtracker web interface:

Running Jobs				
Jobid	Priority	User	Name	Map % Complete
job_201310221656_0020	NORMAL	admin	oozie:action:T=map-reduce:W=wordcount:A=wordcount:ID=0000008-131022165831858-oozie-oozi-W	87.03%

Map Total	Maps Completed	Reduce % Complete	Reduce Total	Reduces Completed	Job Scheduling Information	Diagnostic Info
455	396	0.77%	4	0	NA	NA

- **Completed Jobs**: This section is very similar to that of the running jobs section except that this lists only the completed jobs. This does not show any in-progress or failed jobs.

  The following screenshot shows the **Completed Jobs** section of the jobtracker web interface:

Completed Jobs

Jobid	Priority	User	Name	Map % Complete
job_201310221656_0013	NORMAL	admin	oozie:launcher:T=map-reduce:W=wordcount:A=wordcount:ID=0000005-131022165831858-oozie-oozi-W	100.00%
job_201310221656_0014	NORMAL	admin	oozie:action:T=map-reduce:W=wordcount:A=wordcount:ID=0000005-131022165831858-oozie-oozi-W	100.00%
job_201310221656_0015	NORMAL	admin	oozie:launcher:T=map-reduce:W=wordcount:A=wordcount:ID=0000006-131022165831858-oozie-oozi-W	100.00%
job_201310221656_0017	NORMAL	admin	oozie:launcher:T=map-reduce:W=wordcount:A=wordcount:ID=0000007-131022165831858-oozie-oozi-W	100.00%
job_201310221656_0019	NORMAL	admin	oozie:launcher:T=map-reduce:W=wordcount:A=wordcount:ID=0000008-131022165831858-oozie-oozi-W	100.00%

Map Total	Maps Completed	Reduce % Complete	Reduce Total	Reduces Completed	Job Scheduling Information	Diagnostic Info
1	1	100.00%	0	0	NA	NA
5	5	100.00%	4	4	NA	NA
1	1	100.00%	0	0	NA	NA
1	1	100.00%	0	0	NA	NA
1	1	100.00%	0	0	NA	NA

- **Failed Jobs**: The failed jobs section, as the name suggests, lists all the jobs that failed in the cluster.

  The following screenshot shows the **Failed Jobs** section of the jobtracker web interface:

Failed Jobs

Jobid	Priority	User	Name	Map % Complete	Map Total	Maps Completed
job_201310221656_0010	NORMAL	root	wordcount	100.00%	5	0

Reduce % Complete	Reduce Total	Reduces Completed	Job Scheduling Information	Diagnostic Info
100.00%	4	0	NA	NA

- **Retired Jobs**: The jobs submitted to the Hadoop cluster stay in memory on successful completion. They are automatically written to the disk after a certain configured period of time. This configuration (`mapred.jobtracker.retirejob.interval`) is set in the `mapred-site.xml` file.

The following screenshot shows the **Retired Jobs** section of the jobtracker web interface:

Retired Jobs

Jobid	Priority	User	Name	State
job_201310221656_0011	NORMAL	admin	oozie:launcher:T=map-reduce:W=wordcount:A=wordcount:ID=0000004-131022165831858-oozie-oozi-W	SUCCEEDED
job_201310221656_0007	NORMAL	admin	oozie:launcher:T=map-reduce:W=wordcount:A=wordcount:ID=0000003-131022165831858-oozie-oozi-W	SUCCEEDED
job_201310221656_0005	NORMAL	admin	oozie:launcher:T=map-reduce:W=wordcount:A=wordcount:ID=0000002-131022165831858-oozie-oozi-W	SUCCEEDED

Start Time	Finish Time	Map % Complete	Reduce % Complete	Job Scheduling Information	Diagnostic Info
Tue Nov 19 23:07:32 MST 2013	Tue Nov 19 23:07:41 MST 2013	100.00%	100.00%	NA	NA
Mon Nov 18 15:43:43 MST 2013	Mon Nov 18 15:43:51 MST 2013	100.00%	100.00%	NA	NA
Mon Nov 18 15:17:38 MST 2013	Mon Nov 18 15:17:47 MST 2013	100.00%	100.00%	NA	NA

- **Local Logs**: This section provides hyperlinks to the log directory and the jobtracker history for all the jobs on the cluster. The log directory consists of logs related to the jobtracker as well as tasktracker.

The following screenshot shows the **Local Logs** section of the jobtracker web interface:

One of the hyperlinks of this section is:

- ○ **Job Tracker History**: This hyperlink from the **Local Logs** section brings up the list of all the jobs that ran on the cluster with details of when they were submitted, the ID, the job name, and the user who submitted the job. Here, the job ID is a hyperlink that brings up further details of the job. The following is a screenshot of the **Hadoop Map/Reduce History Viewer** section:

Getting MapReduce job information

The following sections are displayed when the **Jobid** link available in the **Running Jobs** section is clicked:

- **General information**: This section provides basic details of the job such as the user, the name of the job, and the configuration file. Along with this, the section also shows the current status of the job, the running duration, and the job start timestamp.

  The following screenshot shows the general information section:

  ## Hadoop Job 0008 on History Viewer

  User: admin
  JobName: SELECT s07.description, s07.total_emp...DESC(Stage-2)
  JobConf: hdfs://node1.hcluster:8020/user/admin/.staging/job_201403041621_0008/job.xml
  Job-ACLs: All users are allowed
  Submitted At: 4-Mar-2014 21:00:08
  Launched At: 4-Mar-2014 21:00:08 (0sec)
  Finished At: 4-Mar-2014 21:00:18 (10sec)
  Status: SUCCESS
  Analyse This Job

- **Map and reduce progress information**: This section displays the complete details of the number of map and reduce tasks for the current job. Information such as completion status, total number of tasks, number of running tasks, number of completed tasks, and the number of killed tasks are also displayed.

  The following screenshot shows the map and reduce progress information section:

Kind	% Complete	Num Tasks	Pending	Running	Complete	Killed	Failed/Killed Task Attempts
map	99.12%	455	0	4	451	0	0 / 0
reduce	25.79%	4	0	4	0	0	0 / 0

- **Counter information**: Hadoop has several built-in counters that provide information about the job being executed. These counters help us understand the behavior of the job and also assist us identify problems with a job a job. Developers can also build custom counters to track certain aspects of their application. The counter information section provides filesystem counter information, job counter information, and statistics related to the MapReduce operations of the job.

The following screenshot shows the counter information section:

	Counter	Map	Reduce	Total
	FILE: Number of bytes read	0	0	0
	FILE: Number of bytes written	3,493,857,965	2,599,750,035	6,093,608,000
	FILE: Number of read operations	0	0	0
	FILE: Number of large read operations	0	0	0
	FILE: Number of write operations	0	0	0
File System Counters	HDFS: Number of bytes read	4,817,503,685	0	4,817,503,685
	HDFS: Number of bytes written	0	0	0
	HDFS: Number of read operations	930	0	930
	HDFS: Number of large read operations	0	0	0
	HDFS: Number of write operations	0	0	0
	Launched map tasks	0	0	455
	Launched reduce tasks	0	0	4
Job Counters	Data-local map tasks	0	0	435
	Rack-local map tasks	0	0	20
	Total time spent by all maps in occupied slots (ms)	0	0	3,549,298
	Map input records	43,587,430	0	43,587,430
	Map output records	43,587,430	0	43,587,430
	Map output bytes	5,139,170,432	0	5,139,170,432
	Input split bytes	63,245	0	63,245
	Combine input records	0	0	0
	Combine output records	0	0	0
	Reduce input groups	0	0	0
Map-Reduce Framework	Reduce shuffle bytes	0	2,542,075,668	2,542,075,668
	Reduce input records	0	0	0
	Reduce output records	0	0	0
	Spilled Records	43,587,430	0	43,587,430
	CPU time spent (ms)	512,070	72,510	584,580
	Physical memory (bytes) snapshot	73,086,812,160	694,304,768	73,781,116,928
	Virtual memory (bytes) snapshot	290,358,341,632	2,605,297,664	292,963,639,296
	Total committed heap usage (bytes)	44,657,278,976	360,775,680	45,018,054,656
org.apache.hadoop.mapreduce.lib.input.FileInputFormatCounter	BYTES_READ	4,817,440,440	0	4,817,440,440

- **Map and reduce completion graphs**: The map and reduce completion graphs provide a graphical representation of the map and reduce tasks for the job. The map completion graph shows progress information of all the map tasks submitted to the cluster for the job. The reduce completion graph shows progress information of each phase: the copy, sort, and reduce operations.

The following screenshot shows the map and reduce completion graphs:

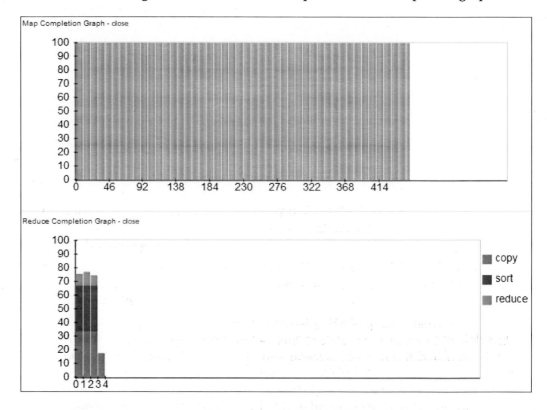

All the preceding information is really helpful to monitor the status of a job.

Summary

In this chapter, we have learned the essentials of HDFS, such as file operations on HDFS and how to configure HDFS. We looked at the namenode and secondary namenode web interfaces and explored a few HDFS commands. We also covered the MapReduce architecture along with a detailed walkthrough of the namenode and jobtracker web interfaces.

In the next chapter, we will dive into **Cloudera's Distribution Including Apache Hadoop (CDH)**.

3
Cloudera's Distribution Including Apache Hadoop

With knowledge of HDFS and MapReduce, you are now ready to explore the world's most used Apache Hadoop distribution, **Cloudera's Distribution Including Apache Hadoop (CDH)**. CDH is thoroughly tested and consists of a host of components that have been carefully packaged to work well with each other.

In this chapter, we will cover the following topics:

- Getting started with CDH
- Understanding the CDH components
- Installing CDH
- Installing the CDH components

Getting started with CDH

Cloudera is an organization that has been working with Hadoop and its related technologies for a few years now. It is an expert in the field of handling large amounts of data using Hadoop and various other open source tools and projects. It is one of the major contributors to several of the Apache projects. Over the years, Cloudera has deployed several clusters for hundreds of its customers. It is equipped with practical knowledge of the issues and details of real production clusters. To solve these issues, Cloudera built CDH.

In most distributed computing clusters, there are several tools that need to work together to provide the desired output. These tools are individually installed and are then configured to work well with each other. This approach often creates problems as the tools are never tested together.

Also, the setup and configuration of these tools is tedious and prone to errors. CDH solves this problem as it is packaged with thoroughly tested tools that work well together in a single powerful distribution. Installation and configuration of the various tools and components is more organized with CDH.

CDH has everything an enterprise needs for its big data projects. The components packaged into CDH provide tools for storage as well as the computation of large volumes of data. By using CDH, an enterprise is guaranteed to have good support from the community for its Hadoop deployment.

Understanding the CDH components

As mentioned earlier, there are several top-level Apache open source projects that are part of CDH. Let's discuss these components in detail.

Apache Hadoop

CDH comes with Apache Hadoop, a system that we have already been introduced to, for high-volume storage and computing. The subcomponents that are part of Hadoop are HDFS, Fuse-DFS, MapReduce, and MapReduce 2 (YARN). Fuse-DFS is a module that helps to mount HDFS to the user space. Once mounted, HDFS will be accessible like any other traditional filesystem.

Apache Flume NG

Apache Flume NG Version 1.x is a distributed framework that handles the **collection** and **aggregation** of large amounts of log data. This project was primarily built to handle streaming data. Flume is robust, reliable, and fault tolerant. Though Flume was built to handle the streaming of log data, its flexibility when handling multiple data sources makes it easy to configure it to handle event data. Flume can handle almost any kind of data. Flume performs the operations of collection and aggregation using agents. An **agent** is comprised of a source, a channel, and a sink.

Events such as the streaming of log files are fed to the source. There are different types of Flume sources, which can consume different types of data. After receiving the events, the sources store the data in channels. A **channel** is a queue that contains all the data received from a source. The data is retained in the channel until it is consumed by the sink. The **sink** is responsible for taking data from channels and placing it on an external store such as HDFS.

The following diagram shows the flow of event/log data to HDFS via the agent:

In the preceding diagram, we see a simple data flow where events or logs are provided as an input to a Flume agent. The source, which is a subcomponent of the agent, forwards the data to one or more channels. The data from the channel is then taken by the sink and finally pushed to HDFS. It is important to note that the source and sink of an agent work asynchronously. The rate at which the data is pushed to the channel and the rate at which the sink pulls the data from the channel are configured to handle spikes that occur with the event/log data.

Using Flume, you can configure more complex data flows where the sink from one agent could be an input to the source of another agent. Such flows are referred to as **multi-hop flows**.

The following diagram shows the flow of event/log data to HDFS via multiple agents:

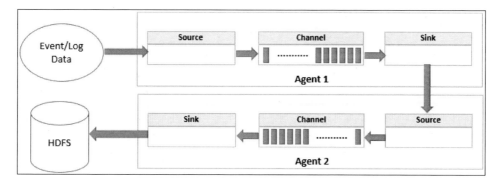

As an administrator, you will appreciate the flexibility of Flume because in many cases, it will be the administrator who recommends solutions to collect and aggregate data to HDFS in a Hadoop cluster.

Apache Sqoop

While analyzing data, data analysts often have to gather data from different sources such as external relational databases and bring it into HDFS for processing. Also, after processing data in Hadoop, analysts may also send the data from HDFS back to some external relational data stores. Apache Sqoop is just the tool for such requirements. Sqoop is used to transfer data between HDFS and relational database systems such as MySQL and Oracle.

Sqoop expects the external database to define the schema for the imports to HDFS. Here, the schema refers to metadata or the structure of the data. The importation and exportation of data in Sqoop is done using MapReduce, thereby leveraging the robust features of MapReduce to perform its operations.

When importing data from an external relational database, Sqoop takes the table as an input, reads the table row by row, and generates output files that are placed in HDFS. The Sqoop import runs in a parallel model (MapReduce), generating several output files for a single input table.

The following diagram shows the two-way flow of data from RDBMS to HDFS and vice versa:

Once the data is in HDFS, analysts process this data, which generates subsequent output files. These results, if required, can be exported to an external relational database system using Sqoop. Sqoop reads delimited files from HDFS, constructs database records, and inserts them into the external table.

Sqoop is a highly configurable tool where you can define the columns that need to be imported/exported to and from HDFS. All operations in Sqoop are done using the command-line interface. Sqoop 2, a newer version of Sqoop, now provides an additional web user interface to perform the importations and exportations.

Sqoop is a client-side application whereas the new Sqoop 2 is a server-side (Sqoop server) application. The Sqoop 2 server also provides a REST API for other applications to easily talk to Sqoop 2.

Apache Pig

Hadoop is a powerful framework. The processing of data in Hadoop is achieved by MapReduce, which is a Java-based framework. All MapReduce applications are written in Java. To make it easier for non-Java programmers to work with Hadoop, Yahoo! developed a platform known as Pig.

Pig, a top-level Apache project, provides a simple high-level scripting language called **Pig Latin**, which allows users to write intuitive scripts to process data stored in HDFS.

Internally, Pig Latin is converted to several MapReduce jobs to process the data in HDFS. Pig is an abstraction over MapReduce.

Apache Hive

Just like Pig, Hive is an abstraction over MapReduce. However, the Hive interface is more similar to SQL. This helps SQL-conversant users work with Hadoop. Hive provides a mechanism to define a structure of the data stored in HDFS and queries it just like a relational database. The query language for Hive is called **HiveQL**.

Hive provides a very handy way to plug in custom mappers and reducers written in MapReduce to perform advanced data processing.

Hive usually runs on the client-side machine. Internally, it interacts directly with the jobtracker daemon on the Hadoop cluster to create MapReduce jobs based on the HiveQL statement provided via the Hive command-line interface. Hive maintains a metastore where it stores all table schemas for the required files stored in HDFS. This metastore is often a relational database system like MySQL.

The following diagram shows the high-level workings of Apache Hive:

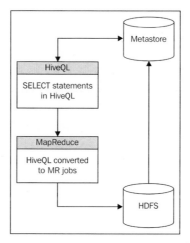

The Hive command-line interface uses the schema available on the metastore along with the query provided, to compute the number of MapReduce jobs that need to be executed on the cluster. Once all the jobs are executed, the output (based on the query) is either displayed onto the client's terminal or is represented as an output table in Hive. The table is nothing but a schema (structure) for the output files generated by the internal MapReduce jobs that were spawned for the provided HiveQL.

Apache ZooKeeper

Building a distributed application requires the management of several nodes and processes working together at the same time. Synchronization and coordination of the nodes is the primary responsibility of any distributed application. As this is a common requirement for many distributed applications, having a common framework to achieve this has been the primary focus of the open source community in the distributed computing space.

Apache ZooKeeper is a distributed coordination service. It is a framework that can be used to build distributed applications by providing a set of services such as a name service, locking, synchronization, configuration management, and leader election services. These services are explained as follows:

- **Name service**: A name service in a distributed systems scenario would be the names and statuses of all the nodes and services in a cluster. ZooKeeper has an in-built mechanism that performs the functions of a name service.

- **Locking**: Often, services in a distributed system will access a single resource at the same time. Locking of the resources allows the sharing of common resources efficiently. ZooKeeper provides a mechanism to lock resources.

- **Synchronization**: ZooKeeper provides a very efficient way of synchronizing access to shared resources on the cluster.

- **Configuration management**: Having a central location for all configuration-related information for nodes in a cluster makes it easy to manage the cluster efficiently. All modifications to the configuration can be done once at the central location, and the changes will be propagated to all nodes in the cluster. Also, when new nodes are added to the cluster, the configuration can be pulled from the central location.

- **Leader election**: Distributed systems are prone to failures whereby nodes crash or fail abruptly. To overcome major cluster downtime, distributed applications usually set up failover nodes for the nodes that could be the single point of failure. ZooKeeper implements the technique of leader election, which works perfectly for such scenarios.

ZooKeeper maintains all its data in a hierarchical structure, just like a traditional filesystem. Each data register (a unit of storage of information) in ZooKeeper is called a **znode** (ZooKeeper node).

A typical ZooKeeper service comprises a set of servers that are used for the replication of information. These multiple servers (**ensemble**) allow ZooKeeper to be highly available, making ZooKeeper itself a distributed application. A client to a ZooKeeper service is the nodes in a cluster. All ZooKeeper information runs in the memory, making it really fast. A copy of the in-memory representation is also maintained on the disk of the server.

The following diagram shows the high-level workings of the ZooKeeper service:

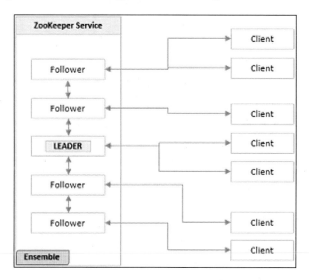

In the preceding diagram, you see a ZooKeeper service with five servers. There is one server that is a leader and four others that are followers. Each client (in a Hadoop cluster, each node in the cluster is a client) connects to exactly one server in the ensemble to read information. The leader is responsible for performing write operations in ZooKeeper. All servers need to know about the other servers in the ensemble.

Once the leader updates the znode with the write operation, the information is propagated to the followers. If the leader server fails, one of the followers becomes a leader and the rest remain followers.

The concept of ZooKeeper will be clearer when we see how Apache Hadoop uses ZooKeeper for namenode high availability. This will be covered in *Chapter 4, Exploring HDFS Federation and Its High Availability*.

Apache HBase

HBase is the Hadoop database. HBase provides fast, random read-write access to a large volume of data. HBase leverages the Hadoop cluster to store large tables that have millions to billions of rows with millions of columns.

HBase is a column-oriented NoSQL data store and was designed based on Google's BigTable implementation. HBase is built on top of HDFS.

Tables in HBase are made of rows and columns. The intersection of a row and column is called a **cell**. The cell in HBase is versioned by applying a timestamp (by default) of when the data was inserted. The row acts as a key for the table, and any access operations on the table are done using the row key.

The following diagram shows the workings of the HBase service:

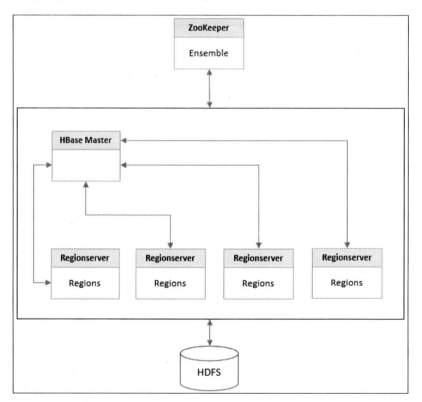

As shown in the preceding diagram, an HBase implementation consists of an HBase master node, which is responsible for managing different RegionServers. When a table in HBase grows in size, it is divided into different regions and is spread across the different nodes of the cluster. Each node that hosts regions is known as **RegionServer**. HBase relies on ZooKeeper to manage the state of the cluster. All important configuration information is stored on the ZooKeeper ensemble. All data for HBase is usually stored in HDFS.

As an administrator, it is very important to know the different components of an HBase cluster as it helps with faster troubleshooting.

Apache Whirr

Organizations that run Hadoop usually set up their hardware infrastructure in-house. However, cloud infrastructure providers such as Amazon and Rackspace allow users to set up a complete cluster in the cloud. Apache Whirr provides the user with a set of libraries/scripts that help users set up and manage a Hadoop cluster on the cloud. As an administrator, you may be tasked with the responsibility of setting up a Hadoop cluster on infrastructure provided by a cloud service provider such as Amazon. If you are given this task, Apache Whirr is the tool that you should be using.

Snappy – previously known as Zippy

In *Chapter 2, HDFS and MapReduce*, we discussed the MapReduce flow in detail. If you recollect, the map phase generates intermediate output files, which are then transferred to reducers for the reduce phase. The output files generated by a map phase can be compressed. The compression allows the intermediate files to be written and read faster. Snappy is a compression/decompression library developed by Google and can be applied to perform the compressions of these output files. Snappy is known for its speed of compression, which in turn improves the speed of the overall operations.

The two properties shown in the following code need to be set in the `mapred-site.xml` file to enable snappy compression during the MapReduce operations:

```
<property>
  <name>mapred.compress.map.output</name>
  <value>true</value>
</property>
<property>
  <name>mapred.map.output.compression.codec</name>
  <value>org.apache.hadoop.io.compress.SnappyCodec</value>
</property>
```

Apache Mahout

Data analysts often apply a few standard, well-established algorithms on their data to generate useful information. When the volumes of data are large like the ones that are available on a Hadoop cluster, they need to be expressed as MapReduce programs. Apache Mahout is a collection of algorithms related to collaborative filtering, clustering, and classification of data. Most of these algorithms have been implemented in MapReduce and are readily available at the disposal of the analysts for their data analysis and processing.

Apache Avro

During the processing of data in a distributed manner, several objects are built and transferred between the nodes of a cluster. These objects are transferred using the process of serialization. **Serialization** is the process of transforming an object in the memory to a stream of bytes. This stream of bytes is then transferred over the wire to the destination node. The destination node reads the stream of bytes and reconstructs the object. This reconstruction is called **deserialization**. Another use of a serialized object is to write it to a persistent store (file). Apache Avro is a serialization-deserialization framework used in Apache Hadoop. In Hadoop, Avro is used for interprocess communication between the different nodes in a cluster.

Apache Oozie

When dealing with big data processing, the task of processing is broken down into several jobs. These jobs need to be executed in a specific sequence to achieve the desired output. Executing these jobs manually would be very tedious. The coordination and scheduling of jobs is called a **workflow**. Apache Oozie is a data workflow management system for Apache Hadoop. Different types of jobs such as MapReduce, Hive, Pig, Sqoop, or custom jobs such as Java programs can be scheduled and coordinated using Oozie.

An Oozie workflow consists of action nodes and control nodes. An action node is a node that executes a specific process, for example, a MapReduce job. Control nodes are nodes that help in controlling the workflow, for example, the start node, end node, and fail node.

The configuration of Oozie workflows is done using **Hadoop Process Definition Language (hPDL)**. hPDL is an XML-based definition language.

The following diagram shows a sample Oozie workflow:

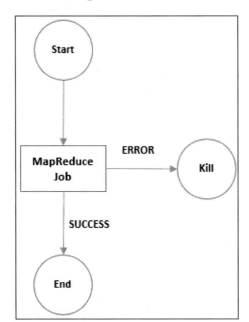

Cloudera Search

Cloudera Search is a search engine for Hadoop. It is a full-text search engine built using Apache Solr, an open source enterprise class search server. The other important components of Cloudera Search are Apache Lucene, Apache SolrCloud, Apache Flume, and Apache Tika. Cloudera Search indexes files stored in HDFS and HBase, making ad hoc analysis on Hadoop super fast.

Cloudera Impala

Cloudera Impala allows users to query data stored in HDFS at real-time speeds. It uses SQL-like query commands similar to that in Apache Hive to query data. Unlike Hive, which is used for long running batch queries, Impala is used for quick data processing and analytics, and also does not create MapReduce jobs to execute queries.

Cloudera Hue

The objective of Cloudera Hue is to make Hadoop more useable. Hue achieves this by eliminating the need to use the command line to operate Hadoop. Hue provides a beautiful web interface with access to all the common tools used for big data processing. Hue is open source.

The following screenshot shows the Cloudera Hue home screen:

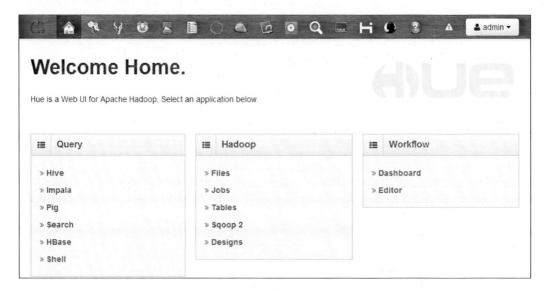

The Hue home is divided into three sections—**Query**, **Hadoop**, and **Workflow**. The **Query** section lists all the tools that could be used to process data stored in the cluster. The **Hadoop** section lists all the administrative tools that deal with the stored data. The **Workflow** section deals with Oozie-related tasks. The links on the three sections can also be accessed using the fixed toolbar on the top of the page.

Beeswax – Hive UI

Beeswax is the Hive UI application that enables users to write HiveQL queries using a web UI. Beeswax allows users to create Hive tables, load data, and execute Hive queries.

The following screenshot shows the Beeswax Hive UI screen:

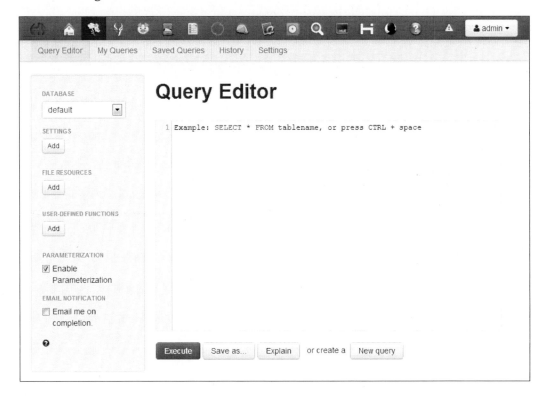

The Hive UI is divided into the following five different tabs:

- The **Query Editor** section, as you can see in the preceding screenshot, has the options to connect to a database along with configurable options to add settings, file resources, and user-defined functions. A large text area is provided to write and execute the query. Options to save and explain the query are also available.

- The **My Queries** section provides the option to view the list of recently saved queries and the recently executed queries.

- The **Saved Queries** section, as the name suggests, displays all the saved queries.

- The **History** section displays all the queries that were executed against the cluster using Hive.

- The **Settings** section displays all the configuration settings for Hive in a tabular format.

Cloudera Impala UI

Hue provides a very simple interface to construct and execute Cloudera Impala queries. The following screenshot shows the Cloudera Impala screen:

The Cloudera Impala UI is almost identical to the Hive UI.

Pig UI

The Pig UI is divided into three tabs:

- The **Editor** section provides all the basic scripting options such as the ability to run and save scripts
- The **Scripts** section provides a list of all the saved Pig scripts
- The **Dashboard** sections display the list of all the running and completed scripts

The following screenshot shows the Pig script editor screen:

File Browser

The File Browser application displays all the files stored in the cluster (HDFS). Users can perform basic file operations such as upload, download, rename, move, copy, and delete. This interface is very handy to quickly browse HDFS. The following screenshot shows the File Browser application's screen:

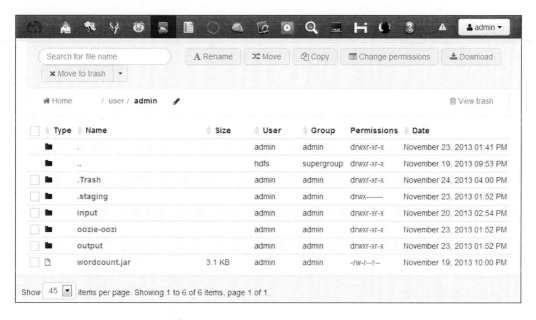

Metastore Manager

The Metastore Manager application is used to perform the following actions:

- Manage the metastore data for Hive and Impala
- Create databases and tables
- Browse data present in the tables

The following screenshot shows the Metastore Manager application's screen:

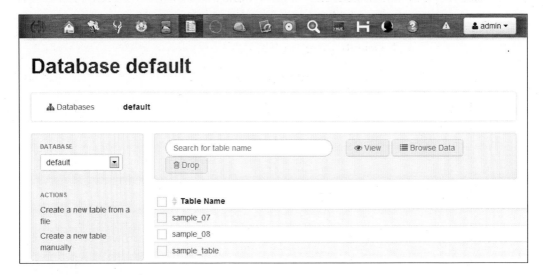

Sqoop Jobs

The **Sqoop Jobs** screen provides a very intuitive interface to build Sqoop jobs. The **New job** link on the top-right corner brings up a simple three-step process screen to build Sqoop jobs.

The following screenshot shows the **Sqoop Jobs** screen:

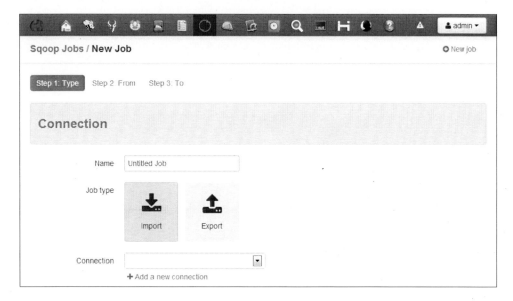

Job Browser

The **Job Browser** screen lists all the jobs that have been executed on the cluster. The list can be filtered on the different status flags: **SUCCEEDED**, **RUNNING**, **FAILED**, and **KILLED**. The **ID** column is a hyperlink, which when clicked, will show more details of that specific job. Details of the job, such as the status, the percentage completions of the maps and reduces, and the duration of the task are also visible. Such information is very useful to monitor jobs submitted to the cluster.

The following screenshot shows the **Job Browser** screen:

Job Designs

The **Job Designs** page allows users to configure different types of jobs such as the MapReduce, Sqoop, Pig, and Hive jobs. Once the jobs are configured, they can be submitted to the cluster. After submission, the status of the jobs can be monitored from the **Job Browser** section.

The following screenshot shows the **Job Designs** screen:

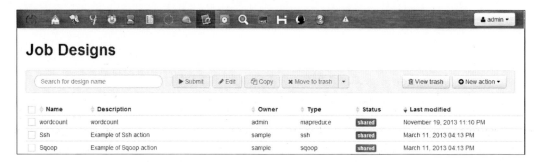

Dashboard

The Oozie Editor/Dashboard is divided into the following four tabs:

- The **Dashboard** section is further divided into dashboards for **Workflows**, **Coordinators**, **Bundles**, and **Oozie**.

  The **Workflows** dashboard section displays the running and completed workflows that were submitted to the cluster. The **Coordinators** dashboard section displays the list of running and completed coordinated jobs that were submitted to the cluster. The Oozie coordinator allows users to configure interdependent workflow jobs. The **Bundle** dashboard section lists all the running and completed bundles that were submitted to the cluster. The **Oozie** section displays the status and configuration parameters of the Oozie workflow system.

- The **Workflows** tab lists all the configured workflows in the system. It also provides the user with an option to create new workflows and manage existing ones.

- The **Coordinators** tab lists all the coordinator applications that have been configured in Oozie. It also provides the user with an option to create new coordinators and manage existing ones.

- Similarly, the **Bundles** tab lists all the bundles configured in Oozie and provides options to create new bundles and manage existing ones.

The following screenshot shows the **Dashboard** screen:

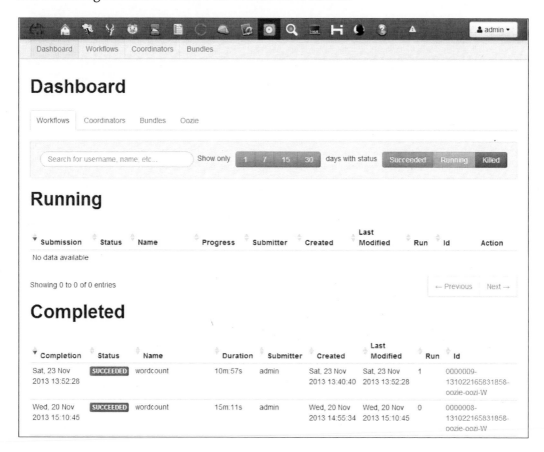

Collection Manager

The **Collection Manager** screen provides the user with the feature to import collections. A collection is basically an index of a dataset. Once the collection is imported, a search can be performed on the collection by navigating to the **Search page** link on the top-right corner.

The following screenshot shows the **Collection Manager** screen:

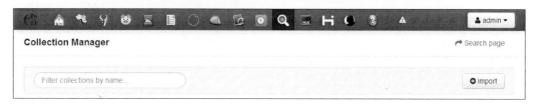

Hue Shell

The Hue Shell provides shell access to Pig, HBase, and Sqoop. For the shell access to work, there should be a Unix user with the same name as that of the Hue user. The following screenshot shows the Hue Shell screen:

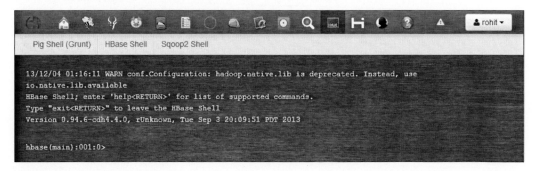

HBase Browser

The **HBase Browser** application lists all the tables that are part of HBase. The user has options to create new tables and manage existing ones.

The following screenshot shows the **HBase Browser** application's screen:

Installing CDH

With a good background knowledge of CDH and its components, let's go ahead and install CDH on a cluster. The remainder of this chapter is going to be hands-on, and we will try to cover everything that is needed to get a fully functional cluster that runs CDH5.

CDH can be installed using one of the following two methods:

- Installation using the operating system's package manager (yum/rpm)
- Installation using Cloudera Manager

In this section, we will cover installation using the operating system's package manager. Installation of CDH using Cloudera Manager will be covered in *Chapter 5, Using Cloudera Manager*.

For the installation, we will be using four servers that run CentOS 6.4 (64-bit) as the operating system.

The following diagram shows a simple four-node Hadoop cluster that runs **MapReduce Version 1 (MRv1)**:

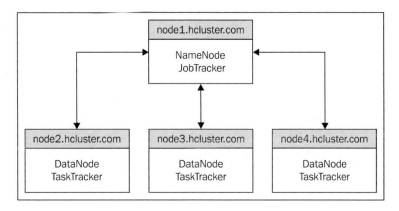

By performing the following installation instructions, we will try to configure our cluster to look like the one shown in the preceding diagram:

1. The first step is to make sure that all our servers are running Oracle Java Version 7. To install Oracle Java, you can download Oracle JDK from Oracle's website. The Oracle Java installation file that I have downloaded is jdk-7u51-linux-x64.rpm. After downloading the file, perform the following instructions as the root user:

   ```
   $ chmod +x jdk-7u51-linux-x64.rpm
   $ rpm -ivh jdk-7u51-linux-x64.rpm
   $ export JAVA_HOME="/usr/java/jdk1.7.0_51/jre/"
   $ export PATH=$JAVA_HOME/bin:$PATH
   ```

   The preceding instructions will install Oracle Java 7, set the JAVA_HOME environment variable, and add the bin folder for the Java runtime to PATH.

2. Create a user, for example, `hduser`, and set a password for the user, using the following commands:

```
$ useradd hduser
$ passwd hduser
```

3. Provide the user with `sudo` privileges by editing the `sudoers` file placed at `/etc` and adding the following line:

```
hduser ALL=(ALL) ALL
```

4. Download the CDH5 RPM for CentOS (here, I am using CentOS 6) using the following link:

```
http://archive.cloudera.com/cdh5/one-click-install/redhat/6/
x86_64/cloudera-cdh-5-0.x86_64.rpm
```

5. Log in as `hduser` and install the downloaded RPM using the following command:

```
$ sudo yum --nogpgcheck localinstall cloudera-cdh-5-0.x86_64.rpm
```

6. Perform steps 1, 2, 3, 4, and 5 on all servers that will be part of the cluster.

7. Execute the following command from the user `hduser` on `node1.hcluster` to install the namenode daemon:

```
$ sudo yum install hadoop-hdfs-namenode
```

8. Execute the following command from the user `hduser` on `node1.hcluster` to install the jobtracker daemon:

```
$ sudo yum install hadoop-0.20-mapreduce-jobtracker
```

9. Execute the following command from the user `hduser` on `node1.hcluster` to install the Hadoop client:

```
$ sudo yum install hadoop-client
```

10. After executing the preceding steps, you will find the file `core-site.xml` under `/etc/hadoop/conf/`. Initially, this file is empty. Edit the file and update it as follows:

```
<?xml-stylesheet type="text/xsl" href="configuration.xsl"?>
<configuration>
  <property>
    <name>fs.defaultFS</name>
    <value>hdfs://node1.hcluster:8020</value>
    <description>
      Defines the name of the filesystem.
    </description>
  </property>
</configuration>
```

For a complete listing of configurable properties for the `core-site.xml` file, refer to `http://hadoop.apache.org/docs/r2.3.0/hadoop-project-dist/hadoop-common/core-default.xml`.

11. Similarly, the file `hdfs-site.xml` under `/etc/hadoop/conf/` will be empty. Update it as follows:

```
<?xml-stylesheet type="text/xsl" href="configuration.xsl"?>
<configuration>
  <property>
    <name>dfs.namenode.servicerpc-address</name>
    <value>node1.hcluster:8022</value>
    <description>
      This is the RPC address for the namenode.
      This address is used by services like the datanodes
      to connect to the namenode.
    </description>
  </property>
  <property>
    <name>dfs.namenode.http-address</name>
    <value>node1.hcluster:50070</value>
    <description>
      This is the HTTP address for the namenode web user
      interface.
    </description>
  </property>
  <property>
    <name>dfs.replication</name>
    <value>3</value>
    <description>
      This property defines the replication factor of the
      data blocks in HDFS.
    </description>
  </property>
  <property>
    <name>dfs.blocksize</name>
    <value>134217728</value>
    <description>
      This property defines block size for files in HDFS
      (bytes).
    </description>
  </property>
</configuration>
```

For a complete list of configurable properties for the `hdfs-site.xml` file, refer to `http://hadoop.apache.org/docs/r2.3.0/hadoop-project-dist/hadoop-hdfs/hdfs-default.xml`.

12. Create the `mapred-site.xml` file in `/etc/hadoop/conf` if is not already present, and update it as follows:

```
<?xml-stylesheet type="text/xsl" href="configuration.xsl"?>
<configuration>
  <property>
    <name>mapred.job.tracker</name>
    <value>node1.hcluster:8021</value>
    <description>
      This property defines the address at which the
      jobtracker service runs.
    </description>
  </property>
  <property>
    <name>mapred.job.tracker.http.address</name>
    <value>0.0.0.0:50030</value>
    <description>
      This property defines HTTP address for jobtracker web
      user interface.
    </description>
  </property>
  <property>
    <name>mapred.reduce.tasks</name>
    <value>4</value>
    <description>
      This property defines the number of reduce tasks that
      can run on the cluster.
    </description>
  </property>
</configuration>
```

For a complete list of configurable properties for the `mapred-site.xml` file, refer to `http://hadoop.apache.org/docs/stable/hadoop-mapreduce-client/hadoop-mapreduce-client-core/mapred-default.xml`.

13. Update the `slaves` file placed at `/etc/hadoop/conf` as follows:

```
node2.hcluster
node3.hcluster
node4.hcluster
```

14. Execute the following command as `hduser` on `node1.hcluster` to format the namenode daemon:

```
$ sudo -u hdfs hdfs namenode -format
```

15. Execute the following command from hduser on node2.hcluster, node3.hcluster, and node4.hcluster to install tasktracker and datanode:

```
$ sudo yum install hadoop-0.20-mapreduce-tasktracker hadoop-hdfs-datanode
```

Copy the core-site.xml, hdfs-site.xml, and mapred-site.xml files from node1.hcluster to node2.hcluster, node3.hcluster, and node4.hcluster in /etc/hadoop/conf/.

16. Execute the following command from hduser on each node to start HDFS:

```
$ for x in 'cd /etc/init.d ; ls hadoop-hdfs-*' ; do sudo service $x start ; done
```

The preceding command will start the namenode daemon on node1.hcluster and the datanode daemon on node2.hcluster, node3.hcluster, and node4.hcluster.

17. Execute the following command from hduser on node1.hcluster:

```
$ sudo -u hdfs hdfs dfs -mkdir /tmp
$ sudo -u hdfs hdfs dfs -chmod -R 1777 /tmp
$ sudo -u hdfs hdfs dfs -mkdir -p /var/lib/hadoop-hdfs/cache/mapred/mapred/staging
$ sudo -u hdfs hdfs dfs -chmod 1777 /var/lib/hadoop-hdfs/cache/mapred/mapred/staging
$ sudo -u hdfs hadoop fs -chown -R mapred /var/lib/hadoop-hdfs/cache/mapred
$ sudo -u hdfs hadoop fs -mkdir /tmp/mapred/system
```

18. Execute the following command from hduser on node1.hcluster to start the jobtracker daemon:

```
$ sudo service hadoop-0.20-mapreduce-jobtracker start
```

19. Execute the following command from hduser on node2.hcluster, node3.hcluster, and node4.hcluster to start the tasktracker daemon:

```
$ sudo service hadoop-0.20-mapreduce-tasktracker start
```

Your four-node Hadoop cluster should now be up and running. You can test the cluster by visiting the URLs for the namenode UI and the jobtracker UI using a browser. The URL for the namenode UI is http://node1.hcluster:50070. The URL for the jobtracker UI is http://node1.hcluster:50030.

To modify the properties of the HDFS and MapReduce, edit the configuration files present under the location /etc/hadoop/conf.

Stopping Hadoop services

Execute the following command from the user `hduser` to stop the namenode daemon on `node1.hcluster` and the datanode daemon on `node2.hcluster`, `node3.hcluster`, and `node4.hcluster`:

```
$ for x in 'cd /etc/init.d ; ls hadoop-hdfs-*' ; do sudo service $x stop
; done
```

Execute the following command from the user `hduser` to stop the jobtracker daemon on `node1.hcluster`:

```
$ sudo service hadoop-0.20-mapreduce-jobtracker stop
```

Execute the following command from the user `hduser` to stop the tasktracker daemon on `node2.hcluster`, `node3.hcluster`, and `node4.hcluster`:

```
$ sudo service hadoop-0.20-mapreduce-tasktracker stop
```

Understanding a YARN cluster

YARN, which also called MRv2, introduces newer daemons that is responsible for job scheduling/monitoring and resource management. Before we go ahead with the installation of YARN, let's look at a typical YARN cluster.

The following diagram shows a simple four-node YARN cluster:

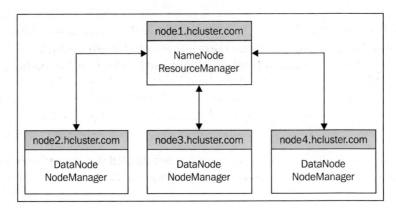

As shown in the preceding diagram, the daemons in a YARN cluster differ from that of an MRv1 cluster. The following list of daemons run as part of a YARN cluster:

- Namenode
- ResourceManager

- Datanode
- NodeManager

Just as we installed MRv1, we can install MRv2 (YARN) on the cluster with a specific set of commands and configuration files. We will go through the installation of MRv2 using a very intuitive and useful application called Cloudera Manager in *Chapter 5, Using Cloudera Manager*.

The previous installation instructions were performed on a very simple four-node cluster to elaborate the installation steps. In real production environments, the number of machines in a cluster range from tens to hundreds of machines.

Installing the CDH components

With a basic Hadoop cluster up and running, we can now install some of the important CDH components.

Installing Apache Flume

To install Apache Flume, log in as `hduser` and execute the following commands:

```
$ sudo yum install flume-ng
$ sudo yum install flume-ng-agent
```

You can configure Apache Flume using the configuration files present under `/etc/flume-g/conf`.

Installing Apache Sqoop

To install Apache Sqoop, log in as `hduser` and execute the following command:

```
$ sudo yum install sqoop
```

You can configure Apache Sqoop using the configuration files present under `/etc/sqoop/conf`.

Installing Apache Sqoop 2

Under Sqoop 2, the services are divided into two parts: `sqoop2-client` and `sqoop2-server`.

To install `sqoop2-server`, log in as `hduser` and execute the following command on one of the nodes in the Hadoop cluster:

```
$ sudo yum install sqoop2-server
```

You can configure the Apache Sqoop2 server using the configuration files present under `/etc/sqoop2/conf`.

To install `sqoop2-client`, log in as `hduser` and execute the following command on any server that you wish to use as a client:

```
$ sudo yum install sqoop2-client
```

Installing Apache Pig

To install Apache Pig, log in as `hduser` and execute the following command:

```
$ sudo yum install pig
```

You can configure Apache Pig using the configuration files present under `/etc/pig/conf`.

Installing Apache Hive

To install Apache Hive, log in as `hduser` and execute the following command:

```
$ sudo yum install hive
```

You can configure Apache Hive using the configuration files present under `/etc/hive/conf`.

Installing Apache Oozie

To install Apache Oozie, log in as `hduser` and execute the following command:

```
$ sudo yum install oozie
```

You can configure Apache Oozie using the configuration files present under `/etc/oozie/conf`.

Installing Apache ZooKeeper

To install Apache ZooKeeper, log in as `hduser` and execute the following command:

```
$ sudo yum install zookeeper-server
```

You can configure Apache Zookeeper using the configuration files present under `/etc/zookeeper/conf`.

With these components installed, you are now ready to use the cluster for data processing. You could use Flume to ingest streaming data from external sources to HDFS, Sqoop or Sqoop 2 to get data from external databases, Pig and Hive to write scripts and queries, and use Apache Oozie to schedule them as required.

There are several other CDH components that can be installed along with the previously mentioned components. However, we will leave the rest and see how they can be installed while going through Cloudera Manager in *Chapter 5, Using Cloudera Manager*.

Summary

In this chapter, we introduced ourselves to CDH and understood the various open source projects that are packaged into CDH. Then we covered the installation of CDH and a few of its components.

In the next chapter, we will discuss HDFS High Availability and HDFS Federation.

4

Exploring HDFS Federation and Its High Availability

You are now ready to set up a Hadoop cluster using CDH5. Once you have a cluster up and running, you are now responsible for managing it and making sure the cluster is available all the time. In this chapter, we will cover some techniques to manage HDFS efficiently and also handle the single point of failure in a Hadoop cluster. In this chapter, we will cover the following topics:

- Configuring HDFS Federation
- HDFS high availability using Quorum-based storage and storage using **Network File System (NFS)**
- Jobtracker high availability

The heart of HDFS is the namenode. The namenode manages the locations of all data blocks in the cluster. To serve requests faster, the namenode manages all its information in memory. For small clusters, the information stored is lightweight and in most cases, a decent amount of RAM is enough to handle all the information required to maintain a cluster. However, when the number of datanodes increases, hosting a large number of files and blocks, the RAM may fall short and would limit the scalability of the cluster. To address this problem, HDFS Federation was built.

Implementing HDFS Federation

HDFS Federation is a technique of splitting up the filesystem namespace into multiple parts. Each part will be managed by an individual namenode, resulting in multiple namenodes.

In the following diagram, you will see two namenodes, **Namenode-1 (NN1)** and **Namenode-2 (NN2)**.

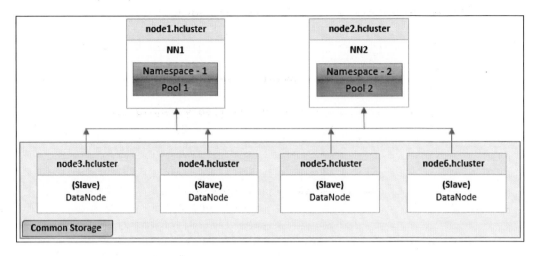

Each namenode manages a namespace volume that consists of the namespace metadata and block pool information. The namespace metadata contains the location information of the files present in HDFS. A block pool is a collection of data blocks that belong to a single namespace in a Hadoop cluster.

Both these namenodes have the same set of datanodes in the cluster. The datanodes store blocks for each of the namenodes. However, the two namenodes do not communicate with each other. In the preceding diagram, you see only two namenodes; however, in production environments, you may have more than two namenodes.

With such architecture in place, it is possible to scale the cluster to a large number of nodes, as the memory is not a limiting factor any more. As a result of this architecture, the read/write operations throughput will significantly improve as the load is not on a single namenode. Having multiple namenodes also provides the ability to isolate operations on the cluster. Operations/applications can be targeted to run on specific namenodes, which could help to segregate the critical ones from the non-critical/experimental ones.

Configuring HDFS Federation

For HDFS Federation to work, the datanodes need a way to identify the different namenodes in the cluster. There are several configuration parameters that need to be added to `hdfs-site.xml`, which are listed in the following table:

Daemon	Configuration Properties
Namenode	`dfs.nameservices`
	`dfs.namenode.rpc-address`
	`dfs.namenode.servicerpc-address`
	`dfs.namenode.http-address`
	`dfs.namenode.https-address`
	`dfs.namenode.keytab.file`
	`dfs.namenode.name.dir`
	`dfs.namenode.edits.dir`
	`dfs.namenode.checkpoint.dir`
	`dfs.namenode.checkpoint.edits.dir`
Secondary namenode	`dfs.namenode.secondary.http-address`
	`dfs.secondary.namenode.keytab.file`

We saw a few of these configuration properties in *Chapter 2*, *HDFS and MapReduce*. The following list defines a few of the important properties used to configure HDFS:

- `dfs.nameservices`: This property defines all the nameservices in the cluster. The nameservice is a name used to uniquely identify an HDFS instance. The values are set as a comma separated list.

- `dfs.namenode.rpc-address`: This property defines the RPC address that handles all client requests.

- `dfs.namenode.https-address`: This property defines the secure HTTP server address for the namenode.

- `dfs.namenode.keytab.file`: This property defines the location of the keytab file. A keytab file is a file that contains principals and encrypted keys. This file is part of the Kerberos configuration, which we will explore in detail a bit later.

- `dfs.namenode.name.dir`: This property defines the location of the fsimage file on the local filesystem. If the value is specified as a comma-separated list of locations, the fsimage file will be replicated on all of the locations for redundancy.

- `dfs.namenode.edits.dir`: This property defines the location of the edits log file. Again, if the value is specified as a comma-separated list of locations, the edits log file will be replicated on all of the locations for redundancy.

- `dfs.namenode.checkpoint.dir`: This property defines the location of the temporary filesystem images to be used by the secondary namenode. If the value is specified as a comma-separated list of locations, the temporary filesystem image file will be replicated on all of the locations for redundancy.

- `dfs.namenode.checkpoint.edits.dir`: This property defines the location of the temporary edits log file to be used by the secondary namenode. If the value is specified as a comma-separated list of locations, the temporary edits log file will be replicated on all of the locations for redundancy.

These properties when configured are suffixed by the **NameserviceID**. For example, assuming that we have two nameservices: *ns1* and *ns2*, there would be two entries in the `hdfs-site.xml` file; one for `dfs.namenode.rpc-address.ns1` and another for `dfs.namenode.rpc-address.ns2`. Let's look at a practical configuration so you understand these properties better.

As shown in the diagram earlier, `node1.hcluster` and `node2.hcluster` are the nodes that will host the namenodes NN1 and NN2 respectively.

The following are the steps to configure HDFS Federation for a new cluster with the two nodes as namenodes (`node1.hcluster` and `node2.hcluster`):

1. Update the `hdfs-site.xml` file to add the following properties:

```
<property>
    <name>dfs.nameservices</name>
    <value>ns1,ns2</value>
  </property>
  <property>
    <name>dfs.namenode.rpc-address.ns1</name>
    <value>node1.hcluster:8020</value>
</property>
  <property>
    <name>dfs.namenode.servicerpc-address.ns1</name>
    <value>node1.hcluster:8022</value>
  </property>
  <property>
```

```
    <name>dfs.namenode.http-address.ns1</name>
    <value>node1.hcluster:50070</value>
</property>
<property>
    <name>dfs.namenode.rpc-address.ns2</name>
    <value>node2.hcluster:8020</value>
</property>
<property>
    <name>dfs.namenode.servicerpc-address.ns2</name>
    <value>node2.hcluster:8022</value>
</property>
<property>
    <name>dfs.namenode.http-address.ns2</name>
    <value>node2.hcluster:50070</value>
</property>
```

2. Copy the updated `hdfs-site.xml` file to all the nodes in the cluster.

3. Format the namenode from user `hduser` on `node1.hcluster` using the following command:

    ```
    $ sudo -u hdfs hadoop namenode -format -clusterId <clusterID>
    ```

4. Specify a unique ID for `<clusterID>`. If this ID is not specified, the unique ID is autogenerated.

5. Format the namenode on `node2.hcluster` using the following command:

    ```
    $ sudo -u hdfs hadoop namenode -format -clusterId <clusterID>
    ```

    Here, the `<clusterID>` is the same ID specified when formatting the namenode on `node1.hcluster`.

> If you are adding federation to an existing cluster, that is, if the namenode on `node1.hcluster` already exists, and you are adding the new namenode on `node2.hcluster`, you only need to format the namenode on `node2.hcluster`. You need to make sure that the cluster ID you use when formatting the namenode on `node2.hcluster` is the same as the one for the namenode on `node1.hcluster`.

6. Start the namenodes on `node1.hcluster` and `node2.hcluster`.

    The two namenodes should now be ready for use in the cluster. We can verify the two namenodes by viewing the cluster web console of the federated cluster at the following URL: `http://node1.hcluster:50070/dfsclusterhealth.jsp`.

As you see in the following screenshot, the two namenodes are listed under the **Namenodes** section. This page also gives a summary that displays the storage information of the cluster.

Cluster ' CID-2b1b5746-f60c-465a-9f51-cb53bf2f1411 '

Cluster Summary

Total Files And Directories : 16
Configured Capacity   : 134.74 GB
DFS Used   : 192 KB
Non DFS Used   : 14.60 GB
DFS Remaining   : 120.15 GB
DFS Used%   : 0.00%
DFS Remaining%   : 89.17%

Namenodes

Number of namenodes : 2

NameNode	Blockpool Used	Blockpool Used%	Files And Directories	Blocks	Missing Blocks	Live Datanode (Decommissioned)	Dead Datanode (Decommissioned)	Software Version
node1.hcluster	120 KB	0.00%	15	1	0	3 (0)	0 (0)	2.3.0-cdh5.0.1
node2.hcluster	72 KB	0.00%	1	0	0	3 (0)	0 (0)	2.3.0-cdh5.0.1

7. To view the namenode on `node1.hcluster`, use the following URL: `http://node1.hcluster:50070/dfshealth.jsp`.

   The following screenshot displays the summary information for `node1.hcluster`. Each namenode will have a common **Cluster ID** but will have a unique **Block Pool ID**.

Overview 'node1.hcluster:8020' (active)

Started:	Fri May 23 21:55:15 MDT 2014
Version:	2.3.0-cdh5.0.1, r8e266e052e423af592871e2dfe09d54c03f6a0e8
Compiled:	2014-05-06T19:01Z by jenkins from (no branch)
Cluster ID:	CID-2b1b5746-f60c-465a-9f51-cb53bf2f1411
Block Pool ID:	BP-2045622565-10.1.3.101-1400900161326

8. To view the namenode on `node2.hcluster`, use the following URL:
   `http://node2.hcluster:50070/dfshealth.jsp`.

   The following screenshot displays the summary information for
   `node2.hcluster`. You will observe that the **Cluster ID** is the same
   as `node1.hcluster`; however, the **Block Pool ID** is different.

Overview 'node2.hcluster:8020' (active)	
Started:	Fri May 23 22:01:36 MDT 2014
Version:	2.3.0-cdh5.0.1, r8e266e052e423af592871e2dfe09d54c03f6a0e8
Compiled:	2014-05-06T19.01Z by Jenkins from (no branch)
Cluster ID:	CID-2b1b5746-f60c-465a-9f51-cb53bf2f1411
Block Pool ID:	BP-328925859-10.1.3.102-1400903971139

The unique **Block Pool ID** number signifies that the namenodes manage their
own block pools and do not interfere with each other's operations. The cluster is
now configured with a federated HDFS. Let's now try to test the two namenodes
using the following steps:

1. Create a folder on the namespace managed by the namenode on
   `node1.hcluster` using the following command:

   ```
   $ sudo -u hdfs hdfs dfs -mkdir hdfs://node1.hcluster:8020/node1_
   data
   ```

2. Create a folder on the namespace managed by the namenode on
   `node2.hcluster` using the following command:

   ```
   $ sudo -u hdfs hdfs dfs -mkdir hdfs://node2.hcluster:8020/node2_
   data
   ```

3. Next, let's list the contents of the two namespaces. To list the contents of the namespace hosted on `node1.hcluster` and `node2.hcluster`, use the commands from the following screenshot:

```
[hduser@node1 ~]$ hdfs dfs -ls hdfs://node1.hcluster:8020/
Found 3 items
drwxr-xr-x   - hdfs supergroup          0 2014-05-23 22:32 hdfs://node1.hcluster:8020/node1_data
drwxrwxrwt   - hdfs supergroup          0 2014-05-23 21:20 hdfs://node1.hcluster:8020/tmp
drwxr-xr-x   - hdfs supergroup          0 2014-05-23 21:16 hdfs://node1.hcluster:8020/var
[hduser@node1 ~]$
[hduser@node1 ~]$ hdfs dfs -ls hdfs://node2.hcluster:8020/
Found 1 items
drwxr-xr-x   - hdfs supergroup          0 2014-05-23 22:33 hdfs://node2.hcluster:8020/node2_data
[hduser@node1 ~]$
```

Configuring ViewFS for a federated HDFS

As you can see for the commands in the preceding screenshot, each namenode was referred to by its name. This is not feasible as each client would need to know the name of each namenode and the files it manages. This is where **ViewFS** comes in. It helps define paths to the different namenodes by using a mount table configuration. The mount table is configured in the `core-site.xml` file.

Edit the `core-site.xml` file by performing the following updates:

1. Update the `fs.defaultFS` property to `viewfs:///` as shown in the following code:

```
<property>
   <name>fs.defaultFS</name>
   <value>viewfs:///</value>
</property>
```

2. Add the following two properties to define the mount points:

```
<property>
   <name>fs.viewfs.mounttable.default.link./n1</name>
   <value>hdfs://node1.hcluster:8020/</value>
</property>
<property>
   <name>fs.viewfs.mounttable.default.link./n2</name>
   <value>hdfs://node2.hcluster:8020/</value>
</property>
```

3. Test the defined mount points by listing the files and folders. The following screenshot shows the list of files in each namenode:

```
[hduser@node1 ~]$ hdfs dfs -ls /n1
Found 3 items
drwxr-xr-x   - hdfs supergroup          0 2014-05-23 22:32 /n1/node1_data
drwxrwxrwt   - hdfs supergroup          0 2014-05-23 21:20 /n1/tmp
drwxr-xr-x   - hdfs supergroup          0 2014-05-23 21:16 /n1/var
[hduser@node1 ~]$ hdfs dfs -ls /n2
Found 1 items
drwxr-xr-x   - hdfs supergroup          0 2014-05-23 22:33 /n2/node2_data
```

The results exactly to the results match the commands using the fully qualified name of the namenode.

The cluster is now ready with a federated HDFS.

Implementing HDFS High Availability

Setting up a cluster is just one of the responsibilities of a Hadoop administrator. Once the cluster is up and running, the administrator needs to make sure the environment is stable and should handle downtime efficiently. Hadoop, being a distributed system, is not only prone to failures, but is expected to fail. The master nodes such as the namenode and jobtracker are single points of failure. A **single point of failure** (SPOF) is a system in the cluster, if it fails, it causes the whole cluster to be nonfunctional. Having a system to handle these single point failures is a must. We will be exploring the techniques on how to handle namenode failures by configuring **HDFS HA (high availability)**.

The namenode stores all the location information of the files in a cluster and coordinates access to the data. If the namenode goes down, the cluster is unusable until the namenode is brought up. Maintenance windows to upgrade hardware or software on the namenode could also cause downtime. The secondary namenode, as we have already discussed, is a checkpoint service and does not support automatic failover for the namenode.

The time taken to bring back the namenode online depends on the type of failure (hardware and software). The downtime could result in **Service Level Agreement (SLA)** slippage as well as the productivity of the data team. To handle such issues and make the namenode more available, namenode HA was built and integrated into Apache Hadoop 2.0.0.

CDH5 comes with HDFS HA built-in. HDFS HA is achieved by running two namenodes for a cluster in an active/passive configuration. In an active/passive configuration, only one namenode is active at a time. When the active namenode becomes unavailable, the passive namenode assumes responsibility and makes itself as the primary active namenode. In this configuration, the two namenodes run on two physically different machines.

The two namenodes in an active/passive configuration are called active namenode and standby namenode respectively. Both the active as well as the standby namenode need to be of similar hardware.

Using CDH5, high availability can be configured using the following two techniques:

- Quorum-based storage
- Shared storage using NFS

The Quorum-based storage

In the Quorum-based storage HA technique, the two namenodes use a **Quorum Journal Manager (QJM)** to share edit logs. As we already know, edits log is the activity log of all file operations on the cluster. Both the active namenode and the standby namenode need to have their edit logs file in sync. To achieve this, the active namenode communicates with the standby namenode using the **JournalNode (JN)** daemons. The active namenode reports every change of its edits logs file to the JournalNodes daemons. The standby namenode reads the edit logs from the JournalNodes daemons and applies all changes to its own namespace. By doing this, the two namenodes are always in sync.

In the following diagram, you see a typical architecture of HDFS HA using QJM. There are two namenodes, active and standby, that communicate with each other via JournalNodes.

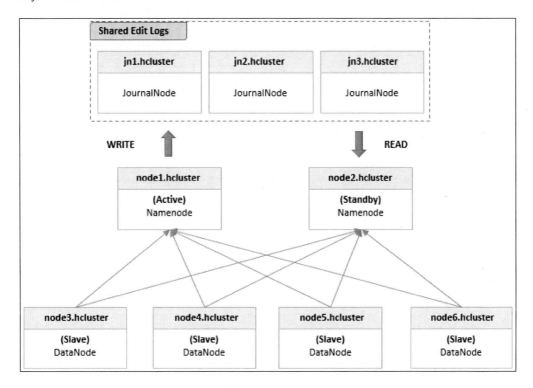

The JournalNodes are daemons that run on JournalNode machines. It is advisable to use at least three JournalNode daemons to make sure the edit logs are written to three different locations allowing JournalNodes to tolerate the failure of a single machine. The system can tolerate the failure of $(N-1)/2$ *JournalNodes*, where N is the number of JournalNodes configured.

At any time, only the active namenode can write to the JournalNodes. This is handled by the JournalNodes to avoid the updates of the shared edit logs by two namenodes, which could cause data loss as well as incorrect results. The standby namenode will only have read access to the JournalNodes to update its own namespace.

When configuring HA, the secondary namenode is not used. As you will recall, the secondary namenode is a checkpoint service that performs periodic checkpoints of the edit logs in the primary namenode and updates the fsimage. The standby namenode in an HA environment performs the checkpoints and does not need a secondary namenode.

The datanodes of the cluster update both the active as well as the standby namenode with the location and heartbeat information, thus making it possible for a quick failover.

When the active namenode fails, the standby namenode assumes the responsibility of writing to the JournalNodes and takes over the active role.

Configuring HDFS high availability by the Quorum-based storage

There are two types of failover configurations: manual failover, which involves manually initiating the commands for failover and automatic failover, where there is no manual intervention.

To configure HDFS HA, a new property, `NamenodeID` is used. The `NamenodeID` is used to distinguish each namenode in the cluster.

Let's look at the properties defined in `hdfs-site.xml` configuration file to set up HDFS HA:

- **dfs.nameservices**: Just as we did for HDFS Federation, we need to configure the nameservices in use for the cluster. For this configuration, I am not using a federated HDFS. The following is a sample configuration entry for `dfs.nameservices`:

```
<property>
  <name>dfs.nameservices</name>
  <value>hcluster</value>
</property>
```

- **dfs.ha.namenodes.[NameserviceID]**: This property defines the unique identifiers for the namenodes in the cluster. The IDs mentioned as values for this property are also referred to as `NamenodeID`. The following is a sample configuration entry for `dfs.ha.namenodes`:

```
<property>
  <name>dfs.ha.namenodes.hcluster</name>
  <value>nn1,nn2</value>
</property>
```

- **dfs.namenode.rpc-address.[NameserviceID].[name node ID]**:
  This property defines the fully qualified RPC address for each configured namenode in the cluster. The following is a sample configuration entry for `dfs.namenode.rpc-address`:

```
<property>
    <name>dfs.namenode.rpc-address.hcluster.nn1</name>
    <value>node1.hcluster:8020</value>
</property>
<property>
    <name>dfs.namenode.rpc-address.hcluster.nn2</name>
    <value>node2.hcluster:8020</value>
</property>
```

- **dfs.namenode.http-address.[NameserviceID].[name node ID]**:
  This property defines the fully qualified HTTP address for each namenode in the cluster. The following is a sample configuration entry for `dfs.namenode.http-address`:

```
<property>
    <name>dfs.namenode.http-address.hcluster.nn1</name>
    <value>node1.hcluster:50070</value>
</property>
<property>
    <name>dfs.namenode.http-address.hcluster.nn2</name>
    <value>node2.hcluster:50070</value>
</property>
```

- **dfs.namenode.shared.edits.dir**: This property defines the URI that identifies the group of JournalNodes to which the NameNodes will read and write edits. The values are a list of the JournalNode addresses. These addresses point to the location where the active namenode writes the edit logs and is subsequently read by the standby namenode. The values are semicolon separated. The following is a sample configuration entry for `dfs.namenode.shared.edits.dir`:

```
<property>
    <name>dfs.namenode.shared.edits.dir</name>
    <value>qjournal://node3.hcluster:8485;node4.hcluster:
8485;node5.hcluster:8485/hcluster</value>
</property>
```

- **dfs.client.failover.proxy.provider.[NameserviceID]**: This property
  defines the Java class that HDFS clients use to contact the active namenode.
  This property helps clients identify the active namenode. Developers can
  write custom classes for this property. The default class that it comes with
  Hadoop is `ConfiguredFailoverProxyProvider`. The following is a sample
  configuration entry for `dfs.client.failover.proxy.provider`:

```
<property>
  <name>dfs.client.failover.proxy.provider.hcluster</name>
  <value>org.apache.hadoop.hdfs.server.namenode.ha.
ConfiguredFailoverProxyProvider</value>
</property>
```

- **fs.defaultFS**: This property defines the default path prefix used by the Hadoop
  FS client when none is given. This property is defined in the `core-site.xml`
  file. The following is a sample configuration entry for `fs.defaultFS`:

```
<property>
  <name>fs.defaultFS</name>
  <value>hdfs://hcluster</value>
</property>
```

- **dfs.journalnode.edits.dir**: This is the complete path of the location where
  the edits and other local state files on the machines running the JournalNode
  service are stored. The following is a sample configuration entry for
  `dfs.journalnode.edits.dir`:

```
<property>
  <name>dfs.journalnode.edits.dir</name>
  <value>/tmp/jnode</value>
</property>
```

Apart from the preceding properties, there are properties that are meant for fencing.
Fencing is a way to assure that only one namenode writes to the JournalNodes.
However, it is possible that when a failover is initiated, the previous active
namenode may still serve client requests till the namenode shuts down. The previous
namenode shuts down when it tries to write to the JournalNodes. Using fencing
methods, this namenode can be shut down as the failover is initiated.

The following are two fencing methods:

- sshfence
- shell

The type of fencing to be used is defined by the `dfs.ha.fencing.methods` property, which is defined by the `hdfs-site.xml` file.

The `sshfence` option provides a way to SSH into the target node and use the `fuser` command to kill the process listening on the TCP port. In other words, it kills the previously active namenode. To perform this action, the SSH needs to happen without a passphrase. For this to work, the `dfs.ha.fencing.ssh.private-key-files` property needs to be configured. The following is a sample configuration entry to set up fencing:

```
<property>
<name>dfs.ha.fencing.methods</name>
<value>sshfence</value>
</property>
<property>
<name>dfs.ha.fencing.ssh.private-key-files</name>
<value>/home/admin/.ssh/id_rsa</value>
</property>
```

In the preceding configuration, we are using the `sshfence` option. The private keys of username, admin, are being used to perform an SSH without passphrase.

Another way to configure `sshfence` would be to use a nonstandard username and port to connect via SSH as shown in the following code:

```
<property>
   <name>dfs.ha.fencing.methods</name>
   <value>sshfence([[username][:port]])</value>
</property>
<property>
   <name>dfs.ha.fencing.ssh.connect-timeout</name>
   <value>30000</value>
</property>
```

A timeout property can be configured to time out the SSH session. If the SSH times out, the fencing mechanism is considered to have failed.

The `shell` fencing option provides a way to run arbitrary shell commands to fence the active namenode as shown in the following code:

```
<property>
   <name>dfs.ha.fencing.methods</name>
   <value>shell(/path/to/my/script.sh –namenode=$target_host
   –nameservice=$target_nameserviceid)</value>
</property>
```

The following is the list of variables with reference to the node that needs to be fenced:

Variable	Description
$target_host	The hostname of the node to be fenced
$target_port	The IPC port of the node to be fenced
$target_address	The combination of the preceding two is configured as <host:port>
$target_nameserviceid	The NameserviceID of the namenode to be fenced
$target_namenodeid	The NamenodeID of the namenode to be fenced

If a fencing method returns 0, the fencing operation is considered successful. Though fencing is not mandatory for HDFS HA using Quorum Journal Manager, it is highly recommended. If no fencing is configured, a default value needs to be set for the property as shown in the following code:

```
<property>
   <name>dfs.ha.fencing.methods</name>
   <value> shell(/bin/true)</value>
</property>
```

Once the configuration files are updated, copy the configurations to all the nodes in the cluster.

Shared storage using NFS

In this approach, the active and standby namenodes need to have access to a common shared storage such as **Network File System** (**NFS**). The active namenode logs a copy of its own namespace modifications on the shared network storage. The standby namenode reads these modifications and applies them to its own namespace and keeps its namespace in sync with the active namenode. In the event of a failover, the standby namenode would have to wait till all the operations from the shared edits log have been applied to its namespace before transitioning into the active state. All datanodes are configured to send to block information and heartbeats to both namenodes. A fencing method needs to be deployed for this approach to make sure that the previously active namenode is shut down before the standby namenode becomes active.

The hardware for the namenode machines in this architecture should be equivalent and just like the hardware setup of a non-HA namenode. The shared storage should be accessible by both the namenodes and should be configured for redundancy to handle failures. Redundancy should be configured for the disk, network, and power. The access and hardware of the shared storage are very critical to this architecture and should be of a high quality with multiple network access paths. Redundancy prevents the NFS (shared storage) from becoming the single point of failure.

Configuring HDFS high availability by shared storage using NFS

Almost all the configuration parameters for the `hdfs-site.xml` configuration file are similar to the one we did for Quorum-based storage. However, we need to update the property as shown in the following code to set up HDFS HA using NFS:

```
<property>
  <name>dfs.namenode.shared.edits.dir</name>
  <value>file:///mnt/shared_storage</value>
</property>
```

Here, the property `dfs.namenode.shared.edits.dir` points to a shared directory, which has been locally mounted.

Once you are done deciding and configuring the desired method for HDFS HA (Quorum-based or Shared Storage), you need to perform the following steps:

1. Stop all Hadoop daemons from `hduser` using the following command on every node:

   ```
   $ for x in 'cd /etc/init.d; ls hadoop*'; do sudo service $x stop ;
   done
   ```

2. Install the namenode package from `hduser` on the node you want to configure as standby. As per our configuration, it is `node2.hcluster`.

   ```
   $ sudo yum install hadoop-hdfs-namenode
   ```

3. If you are using the Quorum-based storage approach, install the JournalNode package from `hduser` on the nodes you want to use as JournalNodes. As per our configuration, we would need to install the JournalNode package on `node3.hcluster`, `node4.hcluster`, and `node5.hcluster`:

   ```
   $ sudo yum install hadoop-hdfs-journalnode
   ```

   This step can be skipped if you are using the Shared Storage approach.

4. Start the JournalNode daemon using the following command on all the nodes where they will run:

```
sudo service hadoop-hdfs-journalnode start
```

In our configuration, the nodes are node3.hcluster, node4.hcluster, and node5.hcluster.

5. Next, go to the primary namenode and execute the following command from hduser to initialize the shared edits directory from the local namenode edits directory:

```
$ sudo -u hdfs hdfs namenode -initializeSharedEdits
```

6. Next, start the primary namenode from hduser using the following command:

```
$ sudo service hadoop-hdfs-namenode start
```

7. Start the standby namenode from hduser using the following command:

```
$ sudo -u hdfs hdfs namenode -bootstrapStandby
$ sudo service hadoop-hdfs-namenode start
```

8. Restart all Hadoop daemons from hduser on all the nodes using the following command:

```
$ for x in 'cd /etc/init.d; ls hadoop*'; do sudo service $x start
; done
```

The preceding steps should start the namenodes on node1.hcluster as well as node2.hcluster along with the other Hadoop daemons. When a namenode starts, it is initially in the standby mode.

Use the hdfs haadmin command to perform the various administrative operations for HDFS HA. To see all the options available with this command, use the hdfs haadmin -help command as shown in the following code:

```
$ hdfs haadmin -help
Usage: DFSHAAdmin [-ns <nameserviceId>]
    [-transitionToActive <serviceId>]
    [-transitionToStandby <serviceId>]
    [-failover [--forcefence] [--forceactive] <serviceId> <serviceId>]
    [-getServiceState <serviceId>]
    [-checkHealth <serviceId>]
    [-help <command>]
```

The following is the description of each option available for the `hdfs haadmin` command:

- **transitionToActive**: This option is used when you want to change the state of a standby namenode to active.

- **transitionToStandby**: This option is used when you want to change the state of an active namenode to standby.

  Usage of the preceding two options is not usually done on production systems as they do not support fencing.

- **failover**: This option is used to perform a failover of the namenodes. Using this flag, the administrator can set the standby namenode to the active state. For our configuration, we can use the following command to set the namenode on `node1.hcluster` to active:

  ```
  $ sudo -u hdfs hdfs haadmin -failover --forceactive nn2 nn1
  ```

  After the namenode enters the standby state, it starts checkpointing the fsimage of the active namenode. The fencing configuration takes effect in case of any failures during failover.

- **getServiceState**: This option is used to print the current status of the namenode. To print the status of the namenodes we have configured, you can use the following commands:

  ```
  $ sudo -u hdfs hdfs haadmin -getServiceState nn1
  $ sudo -u hdfs hdfs haadmin -getServiceState nn2
  ```

- **checkHealth**: This option is used to check the health of the specified namenode. The return value of 0 indicates that the namenode is healthy. A nonzero value is returned if the namenode is unhealthy. As per the current implementation feature, the option will indicate an unhealthy status only if the namenode is down.

The following screenshot shows the summary section of the active namenode:

Overview	'node1.hcluster:8020' (active)
Started:	Sat May 24 18:15:05 MDT 2014
Version:	2.3.0-cdh5.0.1, r8e266e052e423af592871e2dfe09d54c03f6a0e8
Compiled:	2014-05-06T19:01Z by jenkins from (no branch)
Cluster ID:	CID-2b1b5746-f60c-465a-9f51-cb53bf2f1411
Block Pool ID:	BP-2045622565-10.1.3.101-1400900161326

The following screenshot shows the summary section of the standby namenode:

Overview 'node2.hcluster:8020' (standby)	
Started:	Sat May 24 18:19:47 MDT 2014
Version:	2.3.0-cdh5.0.1, r8e266e052e423af592871e2dfe09d54c03f6a0e8
Compiled:	2014-05-06T19:01Z by jenkins from (no branch)
Cluster ID:	CID-2b1b5746-f60c-465a-9f51-cb53bf2f1411
Block Pool ID:	BP-2045622565-10.1.3.101-1400900161326

NameNode Journal Status for Quorum-based storage approach

In the Quorum-based storage approach, only the active namenode will be allowed to perform write operations to the JournalNodes. As shown in the following screenshot, this information is displayed under the **NameNode Journal Status** section:

NameNode Journal Status

Current transaction ID: 31

Journal Manager	State
QJM to [10.1.3.103:8485, 10.1.3.104:8485, 10.1.3.101:8485]	Writing segment beginning at txid 31. 10.1.3.103:8485 (Written txid 31), 10.1.3.104:8485 (Written txid 31), 10.1.3.101:8485 (Written txid 31)
FileJournalManager(root=/var/lib/hadoop-hdfs/cache/hdfs/dfs/name)	EditLogFileOutputStream(/var/lib/hadoop-hdfs/cache/hdfs/dfs/name/current/edits_inprogress_0000000000000000031)

The following screenshot shows the **NameNode Journal Status** of the standby namenode. In the Quorum-based storage approach, the standby namenode is only allowed to perform read operations on the JournalNodes. Also, this information is displayed under the **NameNode Journal Status** section:

NameNode Journal Status

Current transaction ID: 34

Journal Manager	State
QJM to [10.1.3.103:8485, 10.1.3.104:8485, 10.1.3.101:8485]	open for read

Using the preceding steps, an administrator can perform a manual transition from one namenode to the other.

NameNode Journal Status for the Shared Storage-based approach

The following screenshot shows the **NameNode Journal Status** for the standby namenode in the Shared storage-based approach. As you can see in the following screenshot, the standby namenode in the Shared Storage-based approach is only allowed to read from the shared storage:

NameNode Journal Status

Current transaction ID: 87

Journal Manager	State
FileJournalManager(root=/mnt/shared_storage)	open for read

NameNode Storage

Storage Directory	Type	State
/mnt/shared_storage	EDITS	Active
/var/lib/hadoop-hdfs/cache/hdfs/dfs/name	IMAGE_AND_EDITS	Active

As you can see in the following screenshot, the active namenode in a Shared Storage configuration is allowed to write to the common shared location:

NameNode Journal Status

Current transaction ID: 88

Journal Manager	State
FileJournalManager(root=/mnt/shared_storage)	EditLogFileOutputStream(/mnt/shared_storage/current/edits_inprogress_0000000000000000088)
FileJournalManager(root=/var/lib/hadoop-hdfs/cache/hdfs/dfs/name)	EditLogFileOutputStream(/var/lib/hadoop-hdfs/cache/hdfs/dfs/name/current/edits_inprogress_0000000000000000088)

NameNode Storage

Storage Directory	Type	State
/mnt/shared_storage	EDITS	Active
/var/lib/hadoop-hdfs/cache/hdfs/dfs/name	IMAGE_AND_EDITS	Active

Configuring automatic failover for HDFS high availability

To perform an automatic failover where no manual intervention is required, we need to use Apache Zookeeper. As you saw in *Chapter 3, Cloudera's Distribution Including Apache Hadoop*, Apache Zookeeper is a distributed coordination service.

To configure automatic failover, the following two additional components are installed on an HDFS deployment:

- Zookeeper Quorum
- ZK Failover Controller (ZKFC)

The ZooKeeper service is responsible for the following two operations:

- **Failure detection**: The ZooKeeper service is responsible for maintaining a persistent session of the active namenode in the cluster. If the namenode crashes, the session will expire. This will notify the other namenode that a failover needs to be initiated.

- **Active NameNode elections**: ZooKeeper implements the feature of leader election that can be used to elect an active namenode whenever a namenode crashes.

The **ZKFC** component is a ZooKeeper client that helps in monitoring and managing the state of the namenode. A ZKFC service runs on each machine that runs a namenode.

The ZKFC service is responsible for the following operations:

- **Health monitoring**: ZKFC performs namenode health checks by pinging its local namenode periodically and expecting a response. The namenode needs to respond to the ping requests consistently and periodically to communicate its good health status. If the response is not received correctly, the ZKFC considers the namenode to be unhealthy or down.

- **ZooKeeper session management**: This is the most important operation of the ZooKeeper. The namenode maintains a persistent state in ZooKeeper indicating that it is active and healthy. Along with the session information, the namenode also maintains a special znode known as the "lock" znode. As soon as the active namenode fails, the session expires, notifying us that the namenode has failed.

- **ZooKeeper-based election**: The ZKFC constantly checks whether the local namenode is healthy. It constantly keeps an eye on whether there is a lock on the znode held by any other node. If there is no lock, the ZKFC tries to acquire the lock and initiates the failover to set the local namenode as the active namenode.

The ZooKeeper daemons typically run on three or five nodes (number of nodes should be an odd number) and can be collocated with the active and standby namenodes.

Perform the following steps as user `hduser` to configure ZooKeeper for automatic failover:

1. Shut down the entire cluster before configuring ZooKeeper using the following command on every node:

    ```
    $ for x in 'cd /etc/init.d; ls hadoop*'; do sudo service $x stop;
    done
    ```

2. Install ZooKeeper on all the nodes that need to be used as ZooKeeper nodes using the following command:

    ```
    $ sudo yum install zookeeper-server
    ```

3. Start the ZooKeeper service using the following commands:

    ```
    $ sudo service zookeeper-server init --myid=1 --force
    ```

    ```
    $ sudo service zookeeper-server start
    ```

4. Install the ZKFC Failover controller on all nodes that host the namenodes using the following command:

    ```
    $ sudo yum install hadoop-hdfs-zkfc
    ```

5. Update the `hdfs-site.xml` file to include the following property and copy to all the nodes:

    ```
    <property>
      <name>dfs.ha.automatic-failover.enabled</name>
      <value>true</value>
    </property>
    ```

6. Update the `core-site.xml` to include the following property and copy it to all the nodes:

    ```
    <property>
      <name>ha.zookeeper.quorum</name>
      <value>node1.hcluster:2181, node2.hcluster:2181, node3.
    hcluster:2181</value>
    </property>
    ```

7. Initialize the **High Availability (HA)** state in ZooKeeper using the following command from one of the namenodes:

```
$ hdfs zkfc -formatZK
```

This command creates a znode in ZooKeeper, which is used by the automatic failover system to store its data.

8. Restart all Hadoop daemons on all the nodes using the following command:

```
$ for x in 'cd /etc/init.d; ls hadoop*'; do sudo service $x start;
done
```

9. Start the ZooKeeper failover controller on the machines hosting the namenodes using the following command:

```
$ sudo service hadoop-hdfs-zkfc start
```

Your cluster is now configured for automatic failover. You can test this configuration by manually killing the active the namenode using `kill -9` to see if the failover occurs.

Jobtracker high availability

In MRv1, if the jobtracker fails, all running jobs and tasks are lost. Also, the jobtracker service along with its jobs need to be manually restarted. To avoid these issues, the jobtracker needs to be configured for high availability. CDH5 comes inbuilt with the jobtracker HA package.

Configuring jobtracker high availability

Use the following steps from user `hduser` to configure and HA jobtracker for your cluster:

1. Stop all the tasktrackers by executing the following command on all the nodes that host tasktrackers:

```
$ sudo service hadoop-0.20-mapreduce-tasktracker stop
```

2. Stop the jobtracker by executing the following command on the node that hosts the jobtracker:

```
$ sudo service hadoop-0.20-mapreduce-jobtracker stop
```

3. Remove the installed jobtracker using the following command from `node1.hcluster`:

```
$ sudo yum remove hadoop-0.20-mapreduce-jobtracker
```

4. Install the following HA jobtracker package on two independent nodes, which in our case would be node1.hcluster and node2.hcluster:

```
$ sudo yum install hadoop-0.20-mapreduce-jobtrackerha
```

5. If you intend to use automatic failover for the jobtracker, install the ZooKeeper failover controller using the following command on node1. hcluster and node2.hcluster:

```
$ sudo yum install hadoop-0.20-mapreduce-zkfc
```

6. Update the mapred-site.xml file to include the following properties and copy it to all the nodes in the cluster:

```
<property>
  <name>mapred.job.tracker</name>
  <value>myjobtracker</value>
</property>
<property>
  <name>mapred.jobtrackers.myjobtracker</name>
  <value>jt1,jt2</value>
</property>
<property>
  <name>mapred.jobtracker.rpc-address.myjobtracker.jt1
</name>
  <value>node1.hcluster:8021</value>
</property>
<property>
  <name>mapred.jobtracker.rpc-address.myjobtracker.jt2
</name>
  <value>node2.hcluster:8022</value>
</property>
<property>
  <name>mapred.job.tracker.http.address.myjobtracker.jt1
</name>
  <value>0.0.0.0:50030</value>
</property>
<property>
  <name>mapred.job.tracker.http.address.myjobtracker.jt2
</name>
  <value>0.0.0.0:50031</value>
</property>
<property>
  <name>mapred.ha.jobtracker.rpc-address.myjobtracker.jt1
</name>
  <value>node1.hcluster:8023</value>
</property>
```

```
<property>
  <name>mapred.ha.jobtracker.rpc-address.myjobtracker.jt2
</name>
  <value>node2.hcluster:8024</value>
</property>
<property>
  <name>mapred.ha.jobtracker.http-redirect-address.
myjobtracker.jt1</name>
  <value>node1.hcluster:50030</value>
</property>
<property>
  <name>mapred.ha.jobtracker.http-redirect-address.myjobtracker.
jt2
</name>
  <value>node2.hcluster:50031</value>
</property>
<property>
  <name>mapred.ha.fencing.methods</name>
  <value>shell(/bin/true)</value>
</property>
```

7. Start the HA jobtracker daemons on all on the nodes for the jobtrackers. For our configuration, execute the following command on `node1.hcluster` and `node2.hcluster`:

   ```
   $ sudo service hadoop-0.20-mapreduce-jobtrackerha start
   ```

8. If automatic failover is not set up, both jobtrackers will start in the standby state. If you try visiting the URL `http://node1.hcluster:50030/`, the page will be redirected with a message as shown in the following screenshot:

   ## HTTP ERROR 503

   Problem accessing /. Reason:

   ```
   None of the JobTrackers is active
   ```

   Powered by Jetty://

9. To transition jobtracker jt1 to active state, use the following command:

   ```
   $ sudo -u mapred hadoop mrhaadmin -transitionToActive jt1
   ```

Your high available jobtracker is now configured. However, the failover has to be done manually in case the active jobtracker fails.

Configuring automatic failover for jobtracker high availability

To configure automatic failover, use the following steps:

1. Add the following properties to `mapred-site.xml` and copy it to all the nodes in the cluster:

```
<property>
  <name>mapred.ha.automatic-failover.enabled</name>
  <value>true</value>
</property>
<property>
  <name>mapred.ha.zkfc.port</name>
  <value>8018</value>
</property>
```

2. Add the following property to `core-site.xml` file and copy it to all the nodes in the cluster:

```
<property>
  <name>ha.zookeeper.quorum</name>
  <value>node3.hcluster:2181, node4.hcluster:2181, node5.
hcluster:2181 </value>
</property>
```

3. Initialize the HA state of the jobtracker in ZooKeeper using one of the following commands:

```
$ sudo service hadoop-0.20-mapreduce-zkfc init
$ sudo -u mapred hadoop mrzkfc -formatZK
```

4. Enable automatic failover by starting the ZooKeeper failover controller and the HA jobtracker on the jobtracker nodes using the following commands:

```
$ sudo service hadoop-0.20-mapreduce-zkfc start
$ sudo service hadoop-0.20-mapreduce-jobtrackerha start
```

Your cluster is now configured for automatic failover of HA jobtracker. You can test this configuration by manually killing the active jobtracker using `kill -9` to see whether the failover occurs.

With this knowledge, as an administrator, you can now set up a robust highly available Hadoop cluster running CDH5.

Summary

In this chapter, we covered the architecture and implementation of HDFS Federation, which is useful for splitting the namespace into multiple parts and managing them separately. Then we implemented HDFS high availability by configuring two namenodes as an active/passive configuration. We also configured jobtracker high availability by configuring two jobtrackers in an active/passive configuration. Both HDFS HA and jobtracker HA can be configured for manual failover or automatic failover using Apache ZooKeeper.

In the next chapter, we will learn the architecture and implementation of Cloudera Manager, Cloudera's Apache Hadoop administration tool. We will cover all of its features and how it can be used to administer a cluster running CDH5.

Using Cloudera Manager

5

With the knowledge acquired so far, you are now equipped with all the steps and operations needed to set up a cluster via the command line. Up until now, we performed all the operations and configurations manually from the terminal. This is doable when the number of nodes in a cluster is few. But as the number of nodes in a cluster grows, installing CDH and its components manually on all the nodes would be a cumbersome task. Moreover, managing those nodes would be difficult. To solve these problems, Cloudera built **Cloudera Manager**. In this chapter, we will cover the following topics:

- Understanding the architecture of Cloudera Manager
- Installing Cloudera Manager
- Navigating Cloudera Manager Web Console
- Configuring HDFS HA using Cloudera Manager

Introducing Cloudera Manager

Cloudera Manager is a web-browser-based administration tool to manage Apache Hadoop clusters. It is the centralized command center to operate the entire cluster from a single interface. Using Cloudera Manager, the administrator gets visibility for each and every component in the cluster.

A few of the important features of Cloudera Manager are listed as follows:

- It provides an easy-to-use web interface to install and upgrade CDH across the cluster.

- Each node in the cluster can be assigned roles and can be configured accordingly. It allows the starting and stopping of services across all nodes from a single web interface.

- It provides complete information for each node, for example, CPU, memory disk, and network statuses.

Cloudera Manager is available in the following two editions:

- Cloudera Manager Standard (free)
- Cloudera Manager Enterprise (licensed)

Cloudera Manager Standard Edition, though free, is a feature packed tool that can be used to deploy and manage Apache Hadoop clusters with no limitation on the number of nodes. However, there are a few features that are not part of the standard edition. These are as follows:

- **Lightweight Directory Access Protocol (LDAP)** authentication
- Alerts via **SNMP (Simple Network Management Protocol)**
- Operational reports and support integration
- Enhanced cluster statistics
- Disk quota management

These features and a few more are part of the enterprise edition. To get the Cloudera Manager Enterprise Edition, you need to purchase a license. However, as of now, you can try the Enterprise Edition free for 60 days.

Understanding the Cloudera Manager architecture

Before we go into installing and using Cloudera Manager, you need to understand the architecture of Cloudera Manager and how it functions. Cloudera Manager is composed of the following two parts:

- Cloudera Manager Server
- Cloudera Manager Agent

The following diagram depicts the Cloudera Manager architecture:

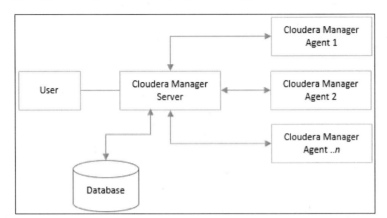

The **Cloudera Manager Server** is the master service that manages the data model of the entire cluster in a database. The data model contains information regarding the services, roles, and configurations assigned for each node in the cluster.

The Cloudera Manager Server is responsible for performing the following functions:

- It communicates with Cloudera Manager Agents that are installed on each node of the cluster and assigns tasks as well as checking the health of each agent by monitoring its periodic heartbeats.

- It provides an administrator web interface for the end user to perform administrator operations.

- It calculates and displays dashboards of the health for the entire cluster.

- It monitors the important parameters such as disk usage, CPU, and RAM for each node in the cluster. It also allows full control on the Hadoop daemons running on the cluster.

- It manages the Kerberos credentials for the services running on the cluster. Kerberos is the tool used to manage the authentication and authorization requirements of the cluster.

- It exposes a set of easy-to-use APIs that helps developers write their own applications to interact with the Cloudera Manager Server.

The Cloudera Manager Agent is installed on each node of the cluster. It is responsible for accepting tasks from the Cloudera Manager Server and performs the starting and stopping of Hadoop daemons on its own node. It is also responsible for gathering all system-level information and statistics and is relayed back to the Cloudera Manager Server.

All communication between the server and its agents is done over HTTP(S). The user also connects to the server using a web browser via HTTP(S). The user uses the web application to perform all the administrator operations.

Installing Cloudera Manager

Cloudera Manager can be installed using the following two methods:

- Automatic installation
- Manual installation

In this section, we will walk through the steps for automatic installation as most of the configurations are handled efficiently by Cloudera Manager itself.

For this demonstration, we will be using the following machine configuration for the Cloudera Manager Server:

- **Operating system**: CentOS 6.4
- **RAM**: 4 GB
- **CPU**: 4 CPU cores
- **Disk space**: 50 GB

For the machines running the Cloudera Manager Agents, we will use the following configuration:

- **Operating system**: CentOS 6.4
- **RAM**: 4 GB
- **CPU**: 4 CPU cores
- **Disk space**: This will depend on the volume of data you want to store in your cluster

For a complete list of all the hardware and software requirements, visit the following Cloudera website:

http://www.cloudera.com/content/cloudera-content/
cloudera-docs/CM4Ent/latest/Cloudera-Manager-
Installation-Guide/cmig_cm_requirements.html

The following are the steps to install Cloudera Manager Server and Cloudera Manager Agents on a cluster:

1. Ensure that all nodes participating in the cluster can communicate with each other over SSH and have their hostnames configured correctly.

2. Download the Cloudera Manager binary from the location at `http://www.cloudera.com/content/support/en/downloads.html`.

3. Once downloaded, modify the downloaded binary file to be executable using the following command:

    ```
    $ chmod u+x cloudera-manager-installer-bin
    ```

4. Next, update the `config` directory under `/etc/selinux` and then set `SELINUX=disabled` to disable **Security-Enhanced Linux (SELinux)**. This is required for the installation of Cloudera Manager and can be re-enabled after installation.

5. Start the installation of Cloudera Manager using the following command:

    ```
    $ ./cloudera-manager-installer-bin
    ```

    As shown in the previous screenshot, the installer starts with the Cloudera Manager **README** screen. The **README** page describes all the steps the Cloudera Manager installer will perform to install the Cloudera Manager Server and its agents. Select **Next** to proceed.

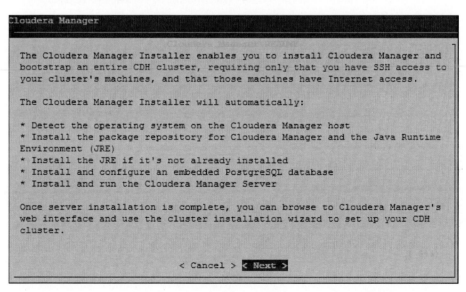

6. You will be presented with the **Cloudera Express License** screen as shown in the following screenshot. Select **Next** to proceed and accept the license.

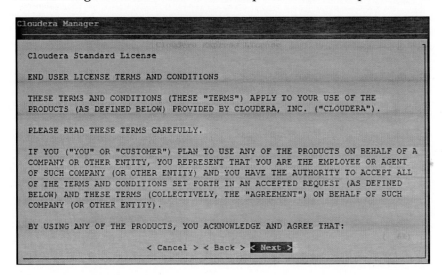

7. On accepting the license, you will be prompted with the **Oracle Binary Code License Agreement**. Select **Next** and accept the license.

8. On accepting the Oracle Binary Code License Agreement, the Cloudera Manager installer starts the installation process, as shown in the following screenshot:

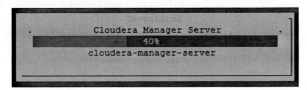

9. After the installation completes, as shown in the following screenshot, a dialog with the URL for the Cloudera Manager Web console is displayed. Click on **OK** and open up a browser to visit the link provided.

```
Point your web browser to http://10.1.3.101:7180/. Log in to Cloudera
Manager with the username and password set to 'admin' to continue
installation. (Note that the hostname may be incorrect. If the url does not
work, try the hostname you use when remotely connecting to this machine.)
If you have trouble connecting, make sure you have disabled firewalls, like
iptables.

                            < OK >
```

10. As shown in the following screenshot, the login screen is displayed for Cloudera Manager. The default username and password is `admin`.

11. The first time you log in, you will be prompted to select the Cloudera Manager edition. We will go ahead and install the Cloudera Enterprise Data Hub Edition Trial version, which can be evaluated for 60 days. This gives us enough time to test out all the features of the full version of Cloudera Manager. If you are interested in getting the Cloudera Manager license, you will need to contact Cloudera directly.

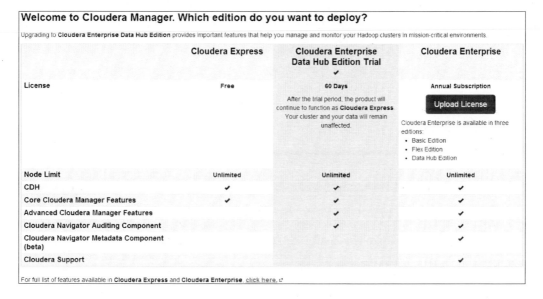

12. The next screen, as shown in the following screenshot, will display the list of services that will be installed as part of Cloudera Enterprise Data Hub Edition Trial 5.0.1. Click on **Continue**.

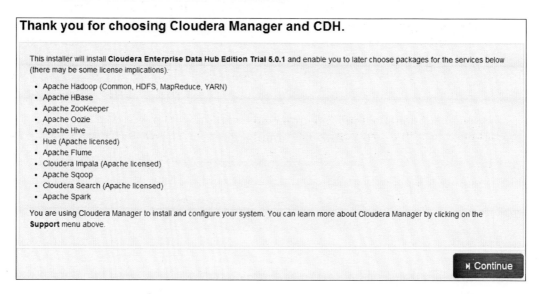

13. In the next step, you will need to enter the hostnames or IP addresses of all machines that are going to be part of your Apache Hadoop cluster. As shown in the following screenshot, you can enter all the addresses and click on **Search** to check whether they are available:

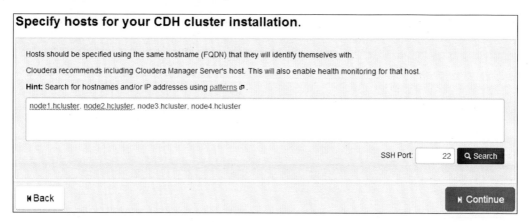

14. After you perform the search, all the machines will be listed as shown in the following screenshot along with the response time from each machine. Once you are satisfied with the results, select the required nodes and click on **Continue**.

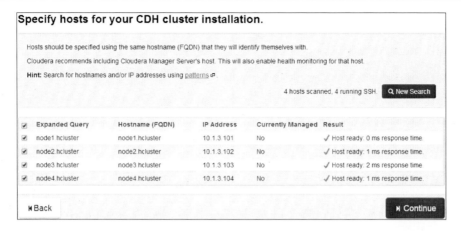

15. After the node selection, you will be presented with a few options to perform the cluster installation as shown in the following screenshot. The cluster installation is a five-step process. The installer provides two types of installation options: packages and parcels. Cloudera recommends the use of parcels. After selecting the required options, click on **Continue**.

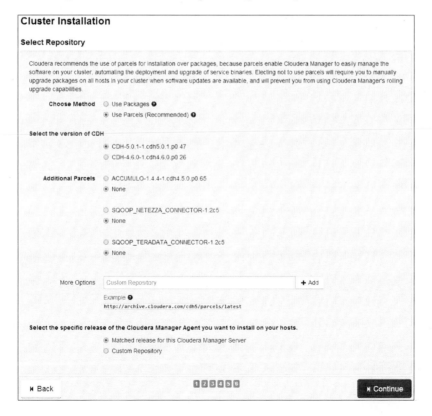

16. The next screen, as shown in the following screenshot, provides an option to install **Java Unlimited Strength Encryption Policy Files**. These files are used to set up a secure server. For now, we can leave the box unchecked and click on **Continue**.

17. Next, provide the SSH username and password to log in to the different machines as shown in the following screenshot. As you can see, we are using the root user. For this set up, the root password is the same for all the nodes in the cluster. Once you are done entering the credentials, click on **Continue**.

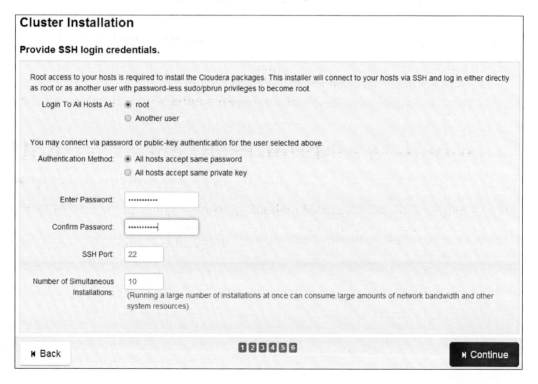

18. The next step starts installing all the Cloudera Manager components to the different machines on the cluster as shown in the following screenshot. This may take a few minutes to complete. If for some reason you want to abort the installation, you can click on **Abort Installation**.

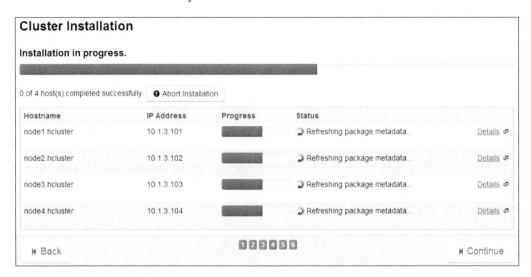

19. After the installation completes, you should see the output as shown in the following screenshot. This confirms that the initial set of Cloudera Manager components have been installed correctly. Also, you will notice that the previously grayed-out **Continue** button is now active. Click on **Continue** to proceed.

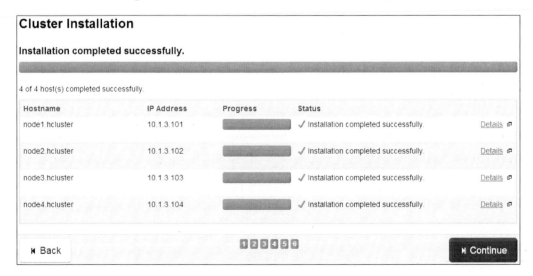

20. After the installation of the initial components of Cloudera Manager, the next step installs the CDH5 parcel as shown in the following screenshot. Once the installation completes, click on **Continue** to proceed.

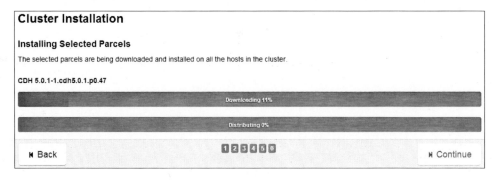

21. After the parcel is installed, all hosts are inspected for correctness as shown in the following screenshot. If there are any errors, a cross mark is displayed next to the failed validation. Click on **Continue** to proceed.

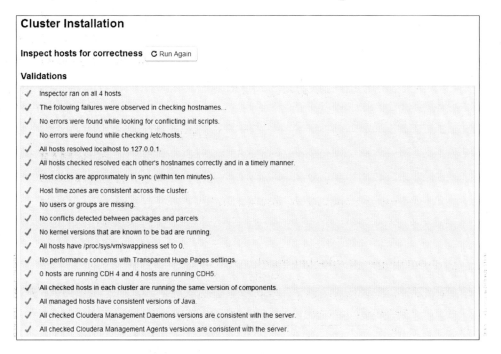

22. The next screen, as shown in the following screenshot, will prompt you to select the different combination of services that you would like to install. Select the appropriate one and click on **Continue**. As you can see, I have selected **All Services** to get all the services available within CDH5 to our cluster.

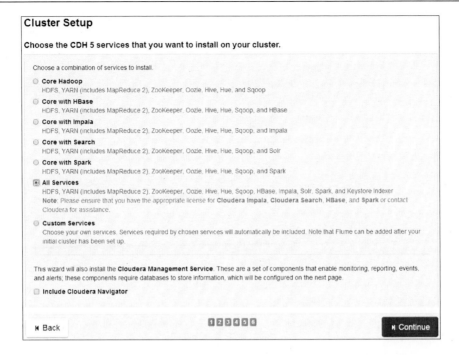

23. The next screen provides the options that can be customized under the **Customize Role Assignments** option.

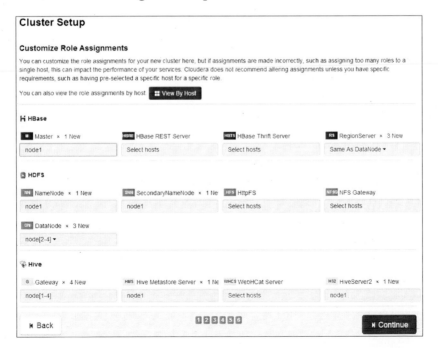

Using this screen, you can decide which services need to run on which hosts. After you are done configuring, click on **Continue**.

24. The next step, as shown in the following screenshot, is to configure the database. We are selecting the **Use Embedded Database** option for our installation. After selecting the option, click on **Test Connection** to test the database connections. Once the connections are successfully tested, the **Continue** button will be activated. Click on **Continue** to proceed.

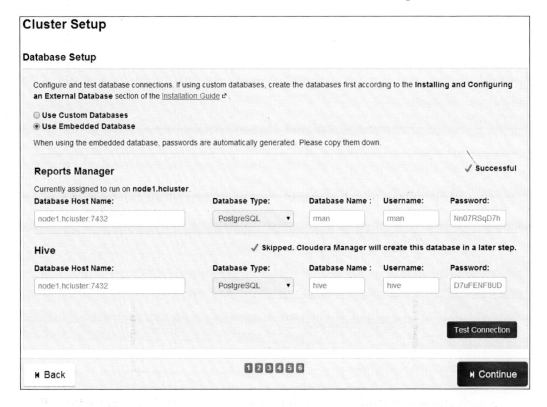

25. The next screen, as shown in the following screenshot, displays all the configuration values for the cluster for review. You can update the values as you desire or leave them at the defaults. Once you are done updating, click on **Continue** to proceed.

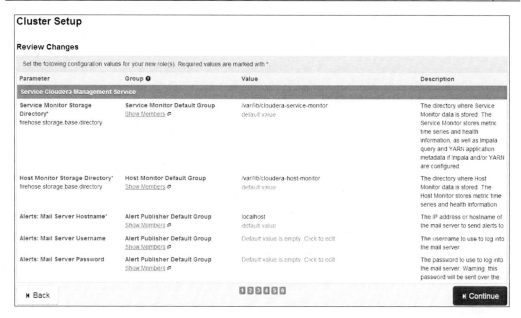

26. The next step, as shown in the following screenshot, starts all the services on the cluster. Once all the services have started successfully, click on **Continue** to proceed.

27. Once the installation is complete, you will be logged in to the Cloudera Manager Administrator Web console as shown in the following screenshot:

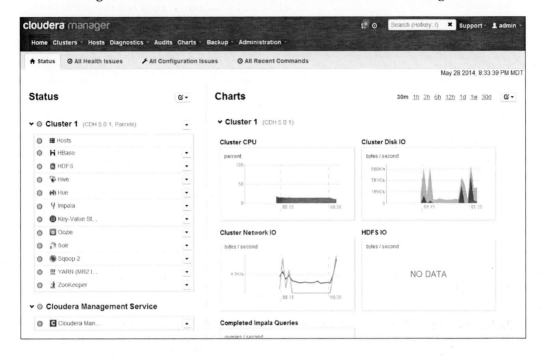

This completes the installation of Cloudera Manager and CDH5 on the cluster. Next, let us look into all the operations available in the Cloudera Manager Web console that could help the administrator manage the Apache Hadoop cluster.

Navigating the Cloudera Manager Web console

The Cloudera Manager Web console is the control center to manage the entire cluster. Once you are logged in to Cloudera Manager, the landing page displays a wealth of information. The different screens can be visited using the Cloudera Manager toolbar as shown in the following screenshot:

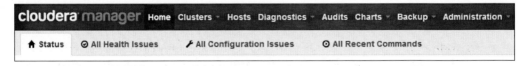

Navigating the Home screen

The **Home** screen is divided into four different tabs, which are as follows:

- This **Status** tab displays the overall status of the cluster with a list of all the components running as shown in the following screenshot. Each service displayed can be started and stopped from this interface.

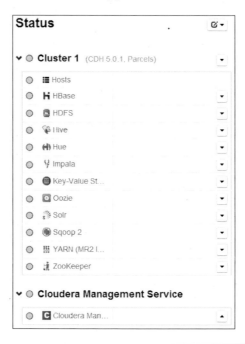

The cluster information is divided into two columns. The first column displays the name of the Hadoop components and the second column displays the important status messages. The circular icon to the left of the component name is the health indicator of the component. The health can be checked by hovering the mouse over the indicator as shown in the following screenshot:

The preceding screenshot indicates that the **ZooKeeper** component has a health concern. The second column gives a few more details indicating that the **ZooKeeper** component has one warning configuration issue. To see the details of these, you can click these indicators, which will pop up the details of the indicator, as shown in the following screenshot. You can further click on the component name to see more details.

The **Status** tab also contains a section that contains charts that display status information of cluster resources. By default, the **Cluster CPU**, **Cluster Disk IO**, **Cluster Network IO**, and **HDFS IO** resources are present on the dashboard, as shown in the following screenshot:

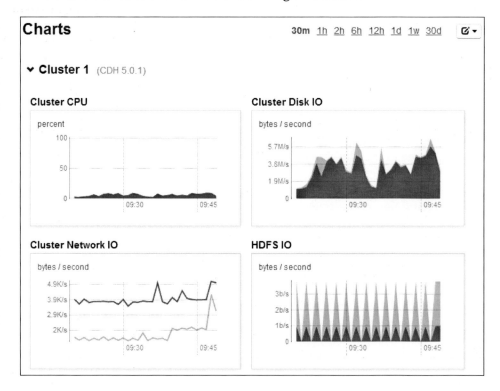

- The **All Health Issues** tab displays the list of components that have health issues as shown in the following screenshot. The screenshot shows that there are two health issues, one for the **hivemetastore** component and one for **jobhistory**. You can see more details by clicking on the individual components listed on the screen as shown in the following screenshot:

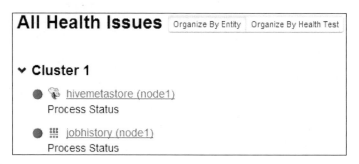

- The **All Configuration Issues** tab displays the list of components that have configuration issues as shown in the following screenshot. The screenshot shows that there are three configuration issues on the cluster. Each issue is described in complete text so you can understand the nature of the issue along with a recommendation. Clicking on any issue will take you to the configuration page of the service and you can resolve the issue there.

All Configuration Issues

❯ **Cluster 1**

○ 🔌 ZooKeeper: **Service zookeeper has 1 Server. Cloudera suggests at least 3 Servers for ZooKeeper.**

○ 🖐 Hue: **Thrift Server role must be configured in HBase service to use the Hue HBase Browser application.**

○ ▦ node1.hcluster: **Memory Overcommit Validation Threshold**
Memory on host node1.hcluster is overcommitted. The total memory allocation is 11.2 GiB bytes but there are only 3.7 GiB bytes of RAM (766.7 MiB bytes of which are reserved for the system). Visit the Resources tab on the Host page for allocation details. Reconfigure the roles on the host to lower the overall memory allocation. Note: Java maximum heap sizes are multiplied by 1.3 to approximate JVM overhead.

- The **All Recent Commands** tab lists all the recent commands executed on the cluster. As you can see in the following screenshot, the recent commands give us information that the ZooKeeper service was recently started:

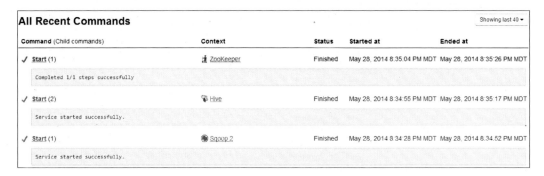

Navigating the Clusters menu

The **Clusters** menu on the Cloudera Manager toolbar displays the list of all services installed on the cluster. The following screenshot shows the menu items of the **Services** menu:

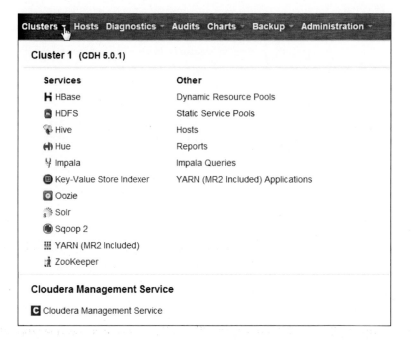

You can click on the services to bring up a detailed view of the selected service. Let us look at one of the services. Each detail window is divided into multiple tabs. For example, if you select the **HDFS** service, the following tabs are displayed:

- **Status**: This tab displays the HDFS summary information along with detailed health information. This page also contains several charts, for example, **HDFS Capacity**, **Total Bytes Read Across DataNodes**, and **Total Bytes Written Across DataNodes**.

- **Instances**: This tab displays the various nodes of the cluster that hosts the HDFS service. Any node that is running the namenode, secondary namenode, or datanode is displayed here along with status, role, and health information.

- **Commands**: This tab displays the list of all the running commands and recent commands executed in relation to the HDFS service.

- **Configuration**: This tab presents a drop-down menu, listing the options to view and edit configurations, role configurations, and an option to view the history of the HDFS configurations along with the configuration options for rollback.

- **Audits**: This tab lists all the actions taken for the HDFS service. This information helps the administrator understand the activities the service is performing. An option to download the audit log is also available.

- **Charts Library**: This tab lists all the charts related to the HDFS service. The page is divided into groups of charts. You will find charts that display information for the entire service along with the ones for the namespace and datanodes.

- **File Browser**: This tab displays the list of files and folders on HDFS.

- **Cache Statistics**: This tab provides the HDFS caching information.

- **Replications**: This tab provides options to configure schedules and sources for HDFS replication and Hive replication.

- **NameNode Web UI**: This tab links to the namenode web interface.

  The following screenshot shows the details for the HDFS service.

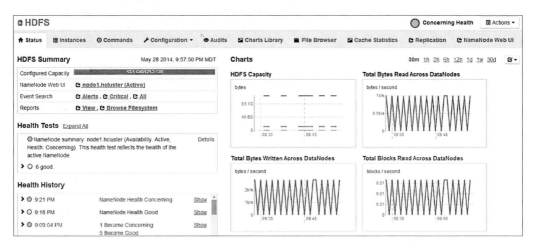

Exploring the Hosts menu

The **Hosts** menu on the Cloudera Manager toolbar displays information of
all the hosts that are part of the cluster. The screen is divided into four tabs:
Status, **Configuration**, **Templates**, and **Parcels**. Let's look into the details of
the latter two tabs here:

- **Templates:** This tab provides the administrator with an option to predefine
  the properties for a specific service or node. For example, a template for the
  TaskTracker can be created with all the required configuration parameters
  and saved. Later on, when the administrator needs to add a new TaskTracker
  in the cluster, he can apply all the required configurations to the new
  TaskTracker using the template.

- **Parcels**: This tab lists all the parcels installed on the cluster along with the
  new parcels available for download. Parcels provide an easy way to install
  the packages on the cluster and it is the Cloudera-recommended method for
  software management.

Understanding the Diagnostics menu

The **Diagnostics** menu on the Cloudera Manager toolbar provides the following three menu items:

- **Events**: This screen displays the list of all the events that occur on the cluster. Three types of events are displayed here: **IMPORTANT**, **INFORMATIONAL**, and **CRITICAL**. As there can be several events that occur, a provision to filter events by the type of events is also available. The following screenshot displays an event with severity—**INFORMATIONAL**. The search can be filtered by other types too, for example, **Content**, **Role**, **Hosts**, **Cluster**, and many more.

- **Logs**: This screen provides a search interface to look into the different logs of services running on the cluster. As shown in the following screenshot, there are several options to search through the logs for specific services. The different services can be selected using the **Select Sources** option.

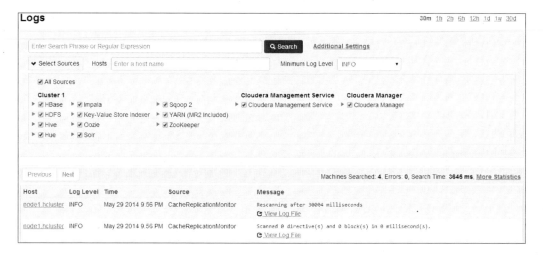

- **Server Log**: The screen displays the Cloudera Manager Server logs as shown in the following screenshot:

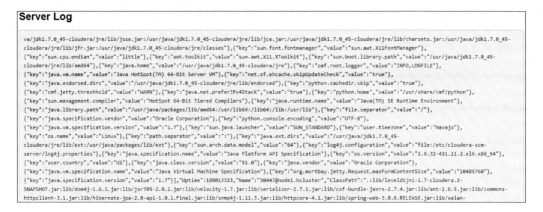

Understanding the Audits screen

The **Audits** menu on the Cloudera Manager toolbar lists all the actions/events performed on the cluster in an easy-to-read format. The interface also provides an option to perform a search on the events using advanced search filters as shown in the following screenshot. The screenshot also shows the list of components available as part of the search filter.

Understanding the Charts menu

The **Charts** menu on the Cloudera Manager toolbar provides an option to create new charts using the **Chart Builder** screen as shown in the following screenshot. You can write a query to select the parameters to create the chart. Once created, you can save the chart.

Understanding the Backup menu

The **Backup** menu provides screens to configure replications for HDFS and Hive data. The menu also provides an option to configure schedules for HDFS and HBase snapshots. We will cover these in detail in *Chapter 9, Configuring Backups*.

Understanding the Administration menu

The **Administration** menu on the Cloudera Manager toolbar contains all the tools required by an administrator to manage the Apache Hadoop cluster. The **Administration** menu has the following items:

- **Settings**: This screen provides an interface to view and edit all the configuration parameters for Cloudera Manager. The properties are divided into multiple groups. The following is a brief description of each of the groups:
    - ○ **Performance**: This group contains the configuration parameters for Cloudera Manager. By default, the only property defined here is the heartbeat interval setting for agents to respond to the server.
    - ○ **Advanced**: This group contains a few properties, such as agent heartbeat logging directory, command data storage directory, and so on. These properties are very rarely modified.
    - ○ **Thresholds**: This group contains properties with respect to the health status check for the agents.

- **Security**: This group contains all the properties related to the security of Cloudera Manager.

- **Ports and Addresses**: This group consists of properties related to the Cloudera Manager services. For example, the hostname, HTTP port for the administrator console, HTTPS port for the administrator console, and the agents port to connect to the server. The following screenshot shows the **Ports and Addresses** group from the **Settings** page:

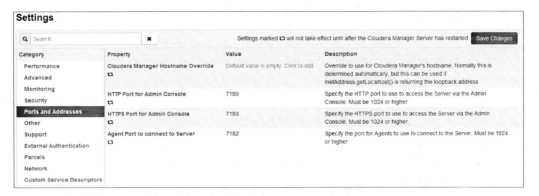

- **Other**: This group consists of few basic properties to configure the look and feel of the Cloudera Manager client.

- **Support**: This group consists of properties related to diagnostic data collection of Cloudera Manager. These properties help configure the frequency and size of the diagnostic data, which can be sent to Cloudera for usage analysis.

- **External Authentication**: This group consists of all the properties related to **Lightweight Directory Access Protocol** (**LDAP**) and **Security Assertion Markup Language** (**SAML**) authentication and authorization.

- **Parcels**: This group contains properties related to parcel package management provided by Cloudera Manager, for example, the parcel local repository directory, remote parcel URLs, and parcel update frequency.

- **Network**: This group provides options to configure the proxy server properties for Cloudera Manager.

- **Custom Service Descriptors**: This group provides options to configure custom add-on services to Cloudera Manager.

- **Alerts**: This screen enables the administrator to configure e-mail alerts for the various services running on the cluster. We will see more of this screen in *Chapter 8, Cluster Monitoring Using Events and Alerts*.

- **Users**: This screen, as the name suggests is the user management console for Cloudera Manager. By default, the admin user is created for Cloudera Manager. Basic user administration activities, such as add/remove the user, manage privileges, and change user passwords is available on this screen.

- **Kerberos**: This screen provides the administrator with options to set up Kerberos, the system to authenticate and authorize users in Apache Hadoop. We will be using this screen to set up Kerberos in *Chapter 6, Implementing Security Using Kerberos*.

- **License**: This screen displays the current license for Cloudera Manager. The following screenshot shows the **License** screen of Cloudera Manager:

As you can see in the preceding screenshot, we are using the trial license for Cloudera Manager. You have the option to stop the trial version using the **End Trial** button or upload a valid enterprise license. The page also displays the current license key along with the license expiry date.

- **Language**: This screen allows you to set the language for Cloudera Manager. The language set here will be the language used for messages such as events and e-mails. The language of Cloudera Manager is derived from the browser's language settings. The following is the screenshot of the **Language** screen in Cloudera Manager:

- **Peers**: This screen provides the administrator with an interface to add peer clusters that are managed by Cloudera Manager. The peer cluster will then become the source from which data, that is, files can be replicated to the currently logged on cluster. Using this feature, you can get files/data (HDFS or Hive data) from a different cluster (peer cluster) and replicate the data in your cluster. The following screenshot shows the **Peers** screen in Cloudera Manager:

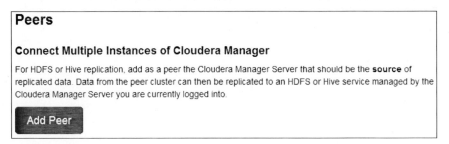

Then, the **Add Peer** screen, shown in the following screenshot, allows you to specify the name of the peer, the peer URL, and the admin credentials of the peer to connect to the peer Cloudera Manager:

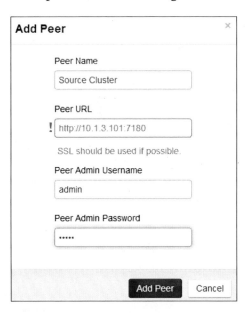

As shown in the following screenshot, once you are done adding the peer, the peer is tested for connectivity and on successful connection, the status is updated to **Connected**:

Configuring High Availability using Cloudera Manager

We know to configure HDFS HA manually using the different commands we learned in *Chapter 4, Exploring HDFS Federation and Its High Availability*. In this section, we will use Cloudera Manager to configure HDFS HA and see how quickly we can set it up just with a few clicks, making the entire process more efficient.

The following are the steps to configure HDFS HA using Cloudera Manager:

1. Log in to Cloudera Manager, navigate to the **Clusters** menu, and select the HDFS service from the **Services** section.

2. Next, click on the **Instances** tab. The screen should look like the one shown in the following screenshot:

3. Click on the **Enable High Availability** button to bring up the four step wizard to configure high availability as shown in the following screenshot:

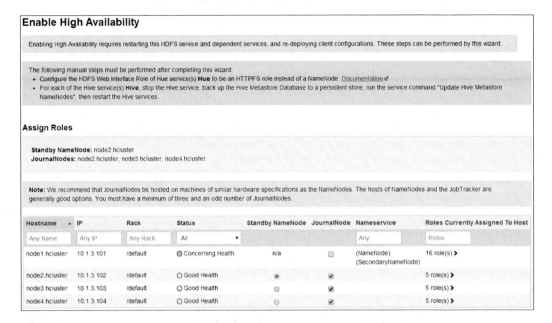

Select the node that will host the standby namenode and the nodes that will host the Journal Node daemons. In the following screenshot, you will see that we have selected `node2.hcluster` to be the standby namenode and `node2.hcluster`, `node3.hcluster`, and `node4.hcluster` to host the Journal Node daemons. After selecting the nodes, click on **Continue**.

4. The next screen provides the option to define the nameservice name as shown in the following screenshot:

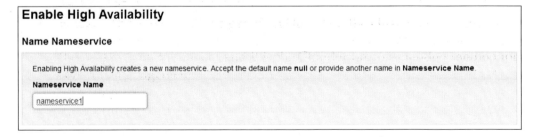

5. In the **Review Changes** screen, you will need to update the values for the **JournalNode Edits Directory** option for all the machines that host the Journal Node daemon. As you can see in the following screenshot, I have set this property to be `/tmp/jndata` for nodes: `node2.hcluster`, `node3.hcluster`, and `node4.hcluster`. After setting these values, click on **Continue**.

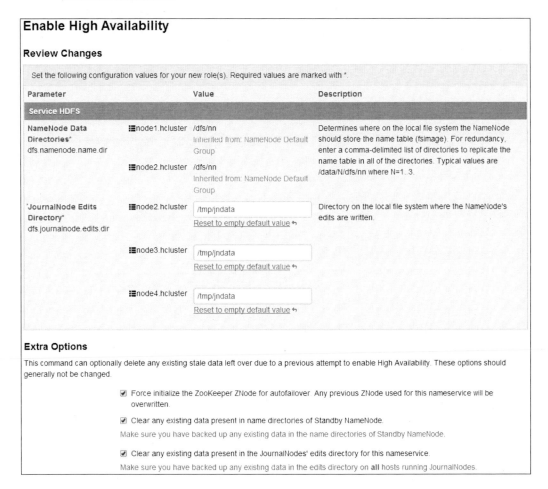

6. In the final step, all the services that require a restart are restarted and the new configuration for clients of the services in the cluster are deployed on the cluster. The following screenshot is a partial screenshot of the successful final step:

Enable High Availability

	Command	Context	Status	Started at	Ended at
✓	Enable High Availability	▣ HDFS	Finished	May 29, 2014 11:37:56 PM MDT	May 29, 2014 11:42:00 PM MDT

Successfully enabled High Availability and Automatic Failover

Command Progress

Completed 20 of 20 steps.

We have successfully configured HDFS HA in six easy steps using Cloudera Manager. This is the real power of Cloudera Manager, which in turn helps the administrator carry out tasks efficiently.

Summary

In this chapter, you were introduced to Cloudera Manager and learned some of its important features. You also got to know about its architecture and how it works with its agents to collect information from the different nodes in the cluster. We then installed Cloudera Manager and navigated the important screens of the web console so you understand its different options and features. We also configured HDFS HA using Cloudera Manager to demonstrate the ease of using Cloudera Manager for administrative activities.

In the next chapter, we will dive into the security aspects of Apache Hadoop, dealing with authentication and authorization of users and services using Kerberos.

6
Implementing Security Using Kerberos

So far, we have covered all that is required to set up an Apache Hadoop cluster running CDH5 and managed by Cloudera Manager. With the cluster now ready to serve large volumes of data to users, the administrator needs to take into account the different users who will be accessing the system. In a production environment, organizations are very stringent in terms of security and expect their data and services to be secure. The administrator needs to have the tools to secure the Apache Hadoop cluster in their armor, and allow only authenticated users to access the cluster. Apart from authorization, the administrator has to be careful about what services in the cluster a user can access. Using **Kerberos**, the administrator can set up a highly secure cluster with robust authentication for users and services.

In this chapter, we will cover the following topics:

- Understanding authentication and authorization
- Introduction to Kerberos
- Understanding the Kerberos architecture
- Installing Kerberos
- Configuring Kerberos for Apache Hadoop
- Configuring Service Level Authorization in Apache Hadoop

Understanding authentication and authorization

In simple terms, authentication is the process of establishing the truth of an entity. Here, the entity could be a user or service on the network. For example, when you log in to your e-mail account, the e-mail server authenticates you based on your username and password. In almost every organization, the users who are part of the organization's network need to be authenticated before they are able to successfully log on to the network. Once the user is authenticated, the user should be restricted to use only the services to which the user is authorized. **Authorization** defines all the resources that a user can access or use. An example of the authorization is clearly visible on a Linux system. Every file and directory has permissions associated with them. These permissions decide which user can read, write, or access the file or directory.

Introducing Kerberos

Kerberos is a network authentication protocol that has been designed to provide a robust authentication solution by employing secret key cryptography. **Massachusetts Institute of Technology (MIT)** has implemented a free version of this protocol, which is widely used.

Kerberos addresses the following requirements:

- Kerberos makes it easy for users to log on and use the different resources on a network without having to go through the login procedure for access to each resource or service. In other words, Kerberos supports single sign-on access that would expect the user to log in only once into the system with seamless authorization to access the rest of the resources.

- Distributed systems involve a large number of nodes connected to form a cluster, just like the Internet we use daily. These nodes could have malicious users that could take advantage of any flaws that exist in the network. Kerberos works well in such environments and protects the network from such users.

- Kerberos is pluggable to any suite of applications without major modifications.

- Kerberos is extremely stringent in terms of data or information transfer and does not perform any exchange unless the requesting user is authenticated as a valid user by Kerberos.

- There are several people who connect to a network with the intention to steal login credentials from other users trying to authenticate to a network. They do this by eavesdropping on the network and extracting passwords that are sent over the wire for authentication. Kerberos is resilient and does not send the password over the wire, thus eliminating the chance of being compromised.

- Kerberos maintains all its authentication-related information in one place and does not maintain it in any distributed fashion across the network. Credential management is more efficient when managed from a single command center.

Let's explore the previously mentioned features of the Kerberos system by getting to know the architecture of the Kerberos protocol.

Understanding the Kerberos Architecture

Before we start configuring Kerberos in a Hadoop environment, we need to get a good understanding of Kerberos and its workings. The following diagram describes the various system components in the Kerberos environment:

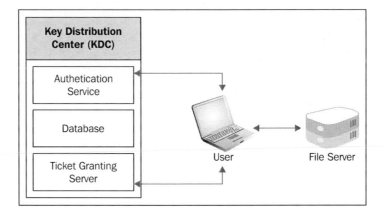

Every Kerberos environment will have a **Key Distribution Center (KDC)**, which is responsible for managing the credentials of users and services in the network. KDC is the centrally located credential store used by Kerberos to authenticate clients.

An example of client would be any user or software service trying to access the network.

As you can seen in the preceding diagram, the KDC is made up of three components:

- **Authentication Service**: This component is responsible for all authentication-related operations
- **Database**: This component stores the secret keys of all the users and services on the network
- **Ticket Granting Server**: This component is responsible for granting the service tickets to users and other services

Using the preceding diagram, let's walk through the entire flow of information during an authentication in a Kerberos environment. To understand it correctly, let's consider a user who needs to access the network and subsequently access a file server on the network.

When a user or service is added to the network, the administrator generates a secret password in the KDC and shares it with the user/service. The secret password is only exchanged during this initial user/service network configuration.

Authenticating a user

In Kerberos, authentication is performed without the user's password being sent over the wire. The following are the sequence of steps to authenticate a user:

1. The user boots up their computer that is connected to the network and enters their credentials (username and password).

2. The computer generates an authenticator packet that is encrypted using the user's password and sends it to KDC. A key thing to note here is that the password is not sent to KDC.

3. When the authenticator packet is received by KDC, it uses the shared secret password to decrypt it. If KDC can decrypt the packet, it trusts this user and provides a **Ticket Granting Ticket** (**TGT**), thus authenticating the user to log in to the network. The TGT has a limited validity period and resides on the user's computer.

4. If the KDC can't decrypt the packet, the user authentication fails, and the user is not allowed to log in to the network.

Accessing a secure file server

Secure access to network services such as file servers is also handled using tickets in Kerberos. The following are the sequence of steps for a user to access a secure file server on the network:

1. The client sends a copy of the TGT with a request to the KDC for a ticket to access the file server.

2. Since the KDC has already authenticated the user, it can easily verify the user as a valid user based on the TGT. The KDC builds a service ticket and encrypts it with the file server's secret key and sends it to the user.

3. The user presents this ticket to the file server. Since the ticket is encrypted using the file server's secret key, the file server is able to decrypt it, thus establishing the trust that it was created by the KDC.

4. The user is granted access to the file server. Any time the user needs to access the file server, the user needs to present the ticket that was generated by the KDC to access the file server.

The KDC stores the shared secret keys of all the users and services on the network. This makes it possible to authenticate the users and services without sending the password over the wire.

Understanding important Kerberos terms

We now have a simplistic view of how the Kerberos protocol works. Next, let's go through some important terms used in a Kerberos environment.

- Any service that has been configured to use Kerberos authentication is said to be **kerberized**.

- **Realm**: A realm is an authentication administrative domain. It defines the network environment. You can think of it as a network domain for authentication, for example, MYREALM.COM.

- **Principal**: A principal is considered to be any entity that has an entry in the KDC database. A principal can be any user, service, or server in the environment defined by the realm. The principal is made up of three parts: primary, instance, and realm.

  ° **Primary**: For a user who is part of the Kerberos configuration, the username will be the primary of the principal, for example, rohitm@MYREALM.COM, where rohitm is the user under the realm MYREALM.COM.

  ° **Instance**: For a user that needs further qualification, an instance can be applied. For example, if you need to qualify the user as an administrator, you as the user principal would look like: rohitm/admin@MYREALM.COM.

  ° **Realm**: For a service running on a host that is part of the Kerberos configuration, the principal would be hdfs/node1.hcluster.com@MYREALM.COM. In this case, we are stating that the principal is the hdfs services running on the host node1.hcluster.com.

- **Keys**: The KDC is the centralized location for all the keys associated with principals on the network. In other words, each principal will have a key in the KDC. This is a shared secret key, that is, only the principal and the KDC are aware of the keys. The key is used to encrypt and decrypt tickets for the purpose of authentication.

- **Keytab**: A keytab is a file that is synonymous to the `/etc/passwd` file that stores user passwords in a Linux system. It contains a list of keys for a specific service. Unlike user principals that use the user's password as the key, a service uses a key generated and stored in a keytab file for authentication. The key in the keytab is a shared secret key that also resides in the KDC.

Installing Kerberos

Before we get started with configuring Kerberos for Apache Hadoop, we need to set up the KDC and the different nodes on the cluster with the required packages.

Configuring the KDC Server

KDC is the Kerberos server and should be the first step in configuring Kerberos on the cluster. The following are the steps to install the server packages:

1. Choose a node on the cluster that you would want to set up as the KDC. Ideally, this node should be used exclusively for the KDC; however, for this demonstration, I am using `node1.hcluster` for the KDC.

2. Install the `krb5-libs`, `krb5-server`, and `krb5-workstation` packages on the KDC node. Use the following commands as the `root` user to install the packages:

```
$ yum install krb5-libs

$ yum install krb5-server

$ yum install krb5-workstation
```

3. Update the `krb5.conf` file in the `/etc/` folder from the `root` user as shown in the following code:

```
[logging]
 default = FILE:/var/log/krb5libs.log
 kdc = FILE:/var/log/krb5kdc.log
 admin_server = FILE:/var/log/kadmind.log

[libdefaults]
```

```
default_realm = MYREALM.COM
dns_lookup_realm = false
dns_lookup_kdc = false
ticket_lifetime = 24h
renew_lifetime = 7d
forwardable = true

[realms]
MYREALM.COM = {
  kdc = node1.hcluster
  admin_server = node1.hcluster
}

[domain_realm]
 .hcluster = MYREALM.COM
 hcluster = MYREALM.COM
```

For our configuration, we are using MYREALM.COM as our realm. In this configuration, node1.hcluster is the KDC.

4. Next, update the kdc.conf files in the /var/kerberos/krb5kdc/ folder from the root user as shown in the following code:

```
[kdcdefaults]
  kdc_ports = 88
  kdc_tcp_ports = 88

[realms]
  MYREALM.COM = {
    master_key_type = aes256-cts
    acl_file = /var/kerberos/krb5kdc/kadm5.acl
    dict_file = /usr/share/dict/words
    admin_keytab = /var/kerberos/krb5kdc/kadm5.keytab
    supported_enctypes = aes256-cts:normal aes128-cts:normal des3-
hmac-sha1:normal arcfour-hmac:normal des-hmac-sha1:normal des-cbc-
md5:normal des-cbc-crc:normal
  }
```

5. Next, we need to get the Java Cryptography Extension policy files from Oracle. These files are needed for our configuration as we are using the **AES256-CTS** type of cryptography for authentication. These policy files are not part of the **Java Runtime Environment (JRE)** by default and need to be explicitly downloaded. The policy files can be downloaded from http://www.oracle.com/technetwork/java/javase/downloads/jce-7-download-432124.html.

6. After downloading the `UnlimitedJCEPolicyJDK7.zip` file, unzip the file to get the following two files:

   ° `local_policy.jar`

   ° `Us_export_policy.jar`

7. On installing Cloudera Manager, Java was installed in `/usr/java/jdk1.7.0_45-cloudera/`. Place the extracted files as the `root` user under the `/usr/java/jdk1.7.0_45-cloudera/jre/lib/security/` directory on all the machines that are part of the cluster. The JDK folder may be different for your installation, so please verify the path before placing the files. You may be prompted to overwrite the existing files. You should choose yes to overwrite the files.

8. Next, we need to set up the database for the KDC. Use `kdb5_util create -s` command as the `root` user as shown in the following screenshot:

```
[root@node1 ~]# kdb5_util create -s
Loading random data
Initializing database '/var/kerberos/krb5kdc/principal' for realm 'MYREALM.COM',
master key name 'K/M@MYREALM.COM'
You will be prompted for the database Master Password.
It is important that you NOT FORGET this password.
Enter KDC database master key:
Re-enter KDC database master key to verify:
[root@node1 ~]#
```

9. Next, update the `kadm5.acl` file in the `/var/kerberos/krb5kdc/` folder from the `root` user as follows:

   `*/admin@MYREALM.COM *`

10. Create the first principal for the `root` user as `root` user using `kadmin.local -q "addprinc root/admin"` command as shown in the following screenshot:

```
[root@node1 ~]# kadmin.local -q "addprinc root/admin"
Authenticating as principal root/admin@MYREALM.COM with password.
WARNING: no policy specified for root/admin@MYREALM.COM; defaulting to no policy
Enter password for principal "root/admin@MYREALM.COM":
Re-enter password for principal "root/admin@MYREALM.COM":
Principal "root/admin@MYREALM.COM" created.
[root@node1 ~]#
```

11. Start the KDC services using the following commands as the `root` user:

```
$ service krb5kdc start
$ service kadmin start
```

The previously mentioned steps should install all the required packages and start the services for KDC.

Testing the KDC installation

It is a good practice to test the KDC server after installation using the following steps:

1. From the machine hosting the KDC service, run the following command to get the ticket granting ticket for the `root` user:

   ```
   $ kinit root/admin@MYREALM.COM
   ```

2. Verify the existence of the **ticket granting ticket** (**TGT**) using the `klist` command as shown in the following screenshot:

```
[root@node1 ~]# klist
Ticket cache: FILE:/tmp/krb5cc_0
Default principal: root/admin@MYREALM.COM

Valid starting        Expires              Service principal
02/08/14 16:11:30   02/09/14 16:11:30   krbtgt/MYREALM.COM@MYREALM.COM
        renew until 02/08/14 16:11:30
[root@node1 ~]#
```

Configuring the Kerberos clients

After configuring the server, we need to set up the clients to work with Kerberos. Following are the steps to install the client packages on all the nodes of the cluster:

1. Install the `krb5-libs` and `krb5-workstation` packages on all the client nodes as a `root` user using the following commands:

   ```
   $ yum install krb5-libs
   $ yum install krb5-workstation
   ```

2. Copy `/etc/krb5.conf` from the KDC server as the `root` user to all the client nodes on the cluster.

The client nodes are now configured to work with Kerberos.

Configuring Kerberos for Apache Hadoop

In this section, we will use Cloudera Manager to configure Kerberos for our cluster running CDH5.

At the time of installation, CDH5 creates the following users:

- hdfs: This user runs the namenode, datanodes, and secondary namenode daemons. The following screenshot shows the hdfs user as the owner of the namenode service:

```
[root@node1 ~]# ps -eaf | grep "proc_namenode"
root      28403 19517  0 12:36 pts/0     00:00:00 grep proc_nam
enode
hdfs      32259  5693  0 Feb05 ?         00:11:27 /usr/java/jdk
1.6.0_31/bin/java -Dproc_namenode -Xmx1000m -Dhdfs.audit.logg
er=INFO,RFAAUDIT -Dsecurity.audit.logger=INFO,RFAS -Djava.net
.preferIPv4Stack=true -Dhadoop.log.dir=/var/log/hadoop-hdfs -
Dhadoop.log.file=hadoop-cmf-hdfs1-NAMENODE-node1.hcluster.log
.out -Dhadoop.home.dir=/opt/cloudera/parcels/CDH-4.5.0-1.cdh4
.5.0.p0.30/lib/hadoop -Dhadoop.id.str=hdfs -Dhadoop.root.logg
er=INFO,RFA -Djava.library.path=/opt/cloudera/parcels/CDH-4.5
.0-1.cdh4.5.0.p0.30/lib/hadoop/lib/native -Dhadoop.policy.fil
e=hadoop-policy.xml -Djava.net.preferIPv4Stack=true -Xms16610
1548 -Xmx166101548 -XX:+UseParNewGC -XX:+UseConcMarkSweepGC -
XX:-CMSConcurrentMTEnabled -XX:CMSInitiatingOccupancyFraction
=70 -XX:+CMSParallelRemarkEnabled -Dhadoop.security.logger=IN
FO,RFAS org.apache.hadoop.hdfs.server.namenode.NameNode
```

- mapred: This user runs the jobtracker and tasktracker daemons when using the MRv1, and job history server daemon when using YARN (MRv2).
- yarn: This user runs the resource manager and node manager daemons.
- oozie: The user runs the Oozie server.
- hue: This user runs the Hue Server, Beeswax Server, Authentication Manager, and Job Designer daemons.

In addition to the preceding users, the Cloudera Manager also creates a user called cloudera-scm. We will need to set up authentication for all of these users in Kerberos.

Configuring Kerberos principal for Cloudera Manager Server

Execute the following steps as the `root` user from `node1.hcluser` to configure the Kerberos principal for Cloudera Manager Server:

1. As shown in the following screenshot, we will use the `kadmin` tool to configure the principal for the `cloudera-scm` user:

```
[root@node1 ~]# kadmin
Authenticating as principal root/admin@MYREALM.COM with password.
Password for root/admin@MYREALM.COM:
kadmin:  addprinc -randkey cloudera-scm/admin@MYREALM.COM
WARNING: no policy specified for cloudera-scm/admin@MYREALM.COM; defaulting to n
o policy
Principal "cloudera-scm/admin@MYREALM.COM" created.
```

2. After creating the principal, we need to create the keytab file for the Cloudera Manager Server as show in the following screenshot:

```
kadmin:  xst -k cmf.keytab cloudera-scm/admin@MYREALM.COM
Entry for principal cloudera-scm/admin@MYREALM.COM with kvno 2, encryption type
aes256-cts-hmac-sha1-96 added to keytab WRFILE:cmf.keytab.
Entry for principal cloudera-scm/admin@MYREALM.COM with kvno 2, encryption type
aes128-cts-hmac-sha1-96 added to keytab WRFILE:cmf.keytab.
Entry for principal cloudera-scm/admin@MYREALM.COM with kvno 2, encryption type
des3-cbc-sha1 added to keytab WRFILE:cmf.keytab.
Entry for principal cloudera-scm/admin@MYREALM.COM with kvno 2, encryption type
arcfour-hmac added to keytab WRFILE:cmf.keytab.
Entry for principal cloudera-scm/admin@MYREALM.COM with kvno 2, encryption type
des-hmac-sha1 added to keytab WRFILE:cmf.keytab.
Entry for principal cloudera-scm/admin@MYREALM.COM with kvno 2, encryption type
des-cbc-md5 added to keytab WRFILE:cmf.keytab.
```

 Here, it is important to note that the Cloudera Manager Server expects the keytab filename to be `cmf.keytab`.

3. Next, copy the `cmf.keytab` file to the `/etc/cloudera-scm-server/` directory on the server where the Cloudera Manager Server is installed.

4. Change the group and user ownership of the `cmf.keytab` file using the following command:

```
$ chown cloudera-scm:cloudera-scm /etc/cloudera-scm-server/cmf.keytab
```

5. Change the permissions for the `cmf.keytab` file, so that `cloudera-scm` user has the read and write permissions on the file. Use the following command to set the permissions:

```
$ chmod 600 /etc/cloudera-scm-server/cmf.keytab
```

6. Create a file named `cmf.prinicpal` and add the following line to the file:

cloudera-scm/admin@MYREALM.COM

7. Place the `cmf.principal` file under the `/etc/cloudera-scm-server/` directory on the server where the Cloudera Manager Server is installed.

8. Change the group and user ownership of the `cmf.principal` file using the following command:

```
$ chown cloudera-scm:cloudera-scm /etc/cloudera-scm-server/cmf.
principal
```

9. Change the permissions for the `cmf.principal` file, so that only the `cloudera-scm` user has the read and write permissions on the file. Use the following command to set the permissions:

```
$ chmod 600 /etc/cloudera-scm-server/cmf.principal
```

Configuring the Cloudera Manager Server for Kerberos

Cloudera Manager provides a simple interface to configure Kerberos for Hadoop. The following are the steps to configure the properties to enable Kerberos security using Cloudera Manager:

1. From the Cloudera Manager Web console navigate to the **Administration | Settings** menu item. Search for the keyword `realm` to bring up the **Kerberos Security Realm** property. Update the property to **MYREALM.COM** and click on **Save Changes**, as shown in the following screenshot:

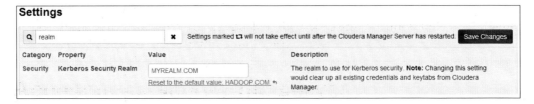

2. Navigate to the home screen of the Cloudera Manager Web console and stop the clusters using the **Stop** menu item as shown in the following screenshot:

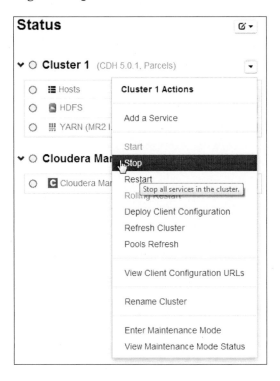

3. Next, stop the **Cloudera Management Service** using the **Stop** menu item as shown in the following screenshot:

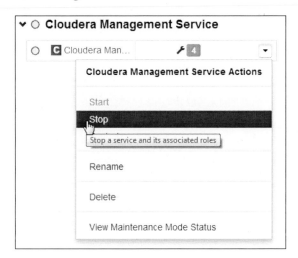

4. On the home screen of the Cloudera Manager Web UI, click on **HDFS**. Navigate to the **Configuration** tab and select the **View and Edit** menu item for **HDFS**. Search for the keyword **Hadoop Secure** and update the properties as shown in the following screenshot:

5. Next, search for the keyword **DataNode**, and update the **DataNode Transceiver Port** and **DataNode HTTP Web UI Port** as shown in the following screenshot:

These values need to be below 1024 and Cloudera recommends 1004 and 1006 for Transceiver port and Web UI port respectively. Click on **Save Changes**.

6. The preceding actions trigger the creation of credentials. To check the status of the generate credentials operation, click on the **Running Commands** icon on the Cloudera Manager toolbar as show in the following screenshot:

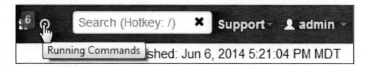

7. You can also check for the status of the operation by clicking on the **All Recent Commands** button on the **Running Commands** screen as shown in the following screenshot:

As you can see in the preceding screenshot, the **Generate Credentials** command has completed successfully.

8. Navigate to **Administration | Kerberos** from the Cloudera Manager Toolbar. You should see the generated credentials as shown in the following screenshot:

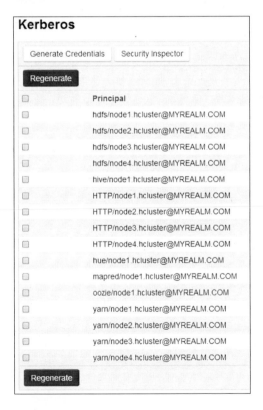

9. From the Cloudera Manager home screen, start the CDH5 cluster and the Cloudera Management service.

10. Once the services start successfully, the cluster starts operating in a secure mode.

11. After the services are kerberized, the access to the `hdfs` superuser is lost and this needs to re-enabled by creating a new `hdfs` user principal as shown in the following screenshot:

```
[root@node1 ~]# kadmin
Authenticating as principal root/admin@MYREALM.COM with password.
Password for root/admin@MYREALM.COM:
kadmin:  addprinc hdfs@MYREALM.COM
WARNING: no policy specified for hdfs@MYREALM.COM; defaulting to no policy
Enter password for principal "hdfs@MYREALM.COM":
Re-enter password for principal "hdfs@MYREALM.COM":
Principal "hdfs@MYREALM.COM" created.
kadmin:
```

The previously mentioned steps complete the Kerberos configuration for CDH using Cloudera Manager. Now, only authorized users can log in to the cluster and only authorized services can communicate with each other.

More details on securing Hadoop clusters can be found at `http://www.cloudera.com/content/cloudera-content/cloudera-docs/CDH5/latest/CDH5-Security-Guide/CDH5-Security-Guide.html`.

Authorization in Apache Hadoop

With authentication, we have validated the user. The next step in the security is to implement Service Level Authorization controls for users. Service Level Authorization sets the permissions for users to the different objects in the cluster. These permissions employ controls on the different actions that a user could perform, for example, submitting a MapReduce job, accessing a file on HDFS, and so on.

Service Level Authorization in Hadoop is done by defining an **access control list (ACL)**. The ACLs allow the administrator to define the list of users that have permissions to the different services in Hadoop.

Configuring access control lists in Hadoop

The ACLs are configured in the `hadoop-policy.xml` file. This file is located under Hadoop's configuration directory. If Cloudera Manager was used to set up CDH on your cluster, you should see this configuration file under the `/opt/cloudera/parcels/<CDH VERSION>/etc/hadoop/conf.dist` directory.

In the cluster, which we are using as examples in this book, the file is present at the `/opt/cloudera/parcels/CDH-5.0.1-1.cdh5.0.1.p0.47/etc/hadoop/conf.dist` directory.

The `hadoop-policy.xml` file consists of name and value pairs for each of the properties. The value is specified as a comma-separated list of users and groups. The user and groups list are separated by a space.

For example, the following value represents an access control list for users, `rohit` and `mark` and for groups, `scientist` and `miners`:

```
<value>rohit, mark scientist, miners</value>
```

By default the value is `*`, which stands for universal access to a service.

The following are a few of the properties:

- `security.client.protocol.acl`: This property defines the access control list for the ClientProtocol interface that is used in user code for job submission. Only the list of users configured in this property will be allowed to talk to the cluster as a distributed filesystem client.

- `security.client.datanode.protocol.acl`: This property defines the access control list for the client to datanode protocol that is used for communication between the client and the datanodes to retrieve data blocks. Only the list of users configured in this property will be allowed to recover blocks from the datanode.

- `security.datanode.protocol.acl`: This property defines the access control list that the datanodes use to communicate with the namenode. Only the list of users configured in this property will be allowed to start the datanodes, which will have access to the namenode.

- `security.namenode.protocol.acl`: Only the list of users configured in this property will be allowed to start the secondary namenode, which will have access to the namenode.

- `security.refresh.policy.protocol.acl`: Only the list of users configured in this property will be allowed to refresh the security policies for Hadoop.

- `security.ha.service.protocol.acl`: Only the list of the users configured in this property will be allowed to perform administration commands required to change the namenode state from active to standby in a high availability scenario.

Summary

In this chapter, we started by understanding authentication and authorization. We also learned the architecture of the Kerberos authentication system, which we installed and configured for Apache Hadoop. We covered the basics of authorization in Apache Hadoop by going through a few of the properties in the `hadoop_policy.xml` file.

In the next chapter, we will cover the tools and techniques to perform all the administrative activities needed to manage a full-fledged Apache Hadoop production cluster.

7
Managing an Apache Hadoop Cluster

We are now equipped with the skills to install and bring up a secure Apache Hadoop cluster running CDH5 and Cloudera Manager. In this chapter, we will learn the different techniques to manage the cluster by covering the following topics:

- Configuring Hadoop services using Cloudera Manager
- Role management in Cloudera Manager
- Managing hosts using Cloudera Manager
- Managing multiple clusters with Cloudera Manager
- Rebalancing an HDFS cluster from Cloudera Manager

Configuring Hadoop services using Cloudera Manager

Cloudera Manager is a very intuitive tool that provides a user-friendly interface to add, remove, and configure services in a cluster. In this section, we will cover the addition and removal of services in a cluster.

Adding a service to the cluster

The following are the steps to add a service to the cluster:

1. Log in to Cloudera Manager. The **Home** screen lists all the services that are currently installed on the cluster as shown in the following screenshot:

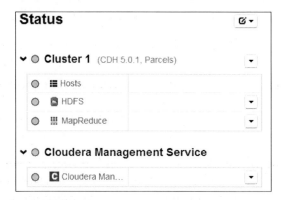

2. In the preceding screenshot, there are only two services in **Cluster 1**. Let's now add the Hive service to this cluster. To add Hive, click on the drop-down button for **Cluster 1** and select the **Add a Service** option as shown in the following screenshot:

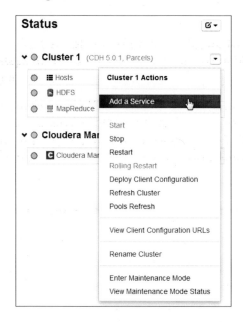

In the next screen, a list of service types along with their description is displayed, as shown in the following screenshot:

3. To add the Hive service (the data warehouse system for Hadoop), select **Hive** from the list and click on **Continue**.

4. Next, select the dependencies for the Hive service as shown in the following screenshot; in this case, select **hdfs** and click on **Continue**:

5. On the next screen, you are given the option to select hosts for the **Hive Metastore** and the **Hive Gateway**. The Hive Metastore is responsible for storing the metadata of the Hive schemas, tables, and partitions. The Hive Gateway is where you can host the Hive shell client. Cloudera Manager, by default, selects a host automatically.

The role assignment screen is shown in the following screenshot. Click on **Continue**.

6. The next screen, as shown in the following screenshot, provides the options to select the database for the Hive Metastore:

There are two types of databases you can create for the Hive Metastore:

° **Embedded**: On selecting **Use Embedded Database**, a PostgreSQL database will be automatically created and managed by Cloudera Manager to store the Hive Metastore

° **Custom**: On selecting **Use Custom Database**, all the database details have to be provided by the administrator

For this demonstration, let's select **Use Embedded Database**. Copy down the generated password for future reference and click on the **Test Connection** button to test the database connection. After the testing operation completes, click on **Continue**.

7. The next screen, as shown in the following screenshot, displays the default configuration changes for review. Click on **Continue** to proceed.

8. In the next step, we perform all the required actions to set up the Hive service on the cluster. The following screenshot shows the different actions Cloudera Manager performs to set up Hive. Once the steps are complete, click on **Continue**.

9. Once the service is successfully set up, you should see a message as shown in the following screenshot. Click on the **Finish** button to complete the setup.

10. You should now see the newly configured Hive service on the **Home** page as shown in the following screenshot:

Using the preceding steps, we have successfully set up Hive on the cluster. The steps are almost identical to add any other service to the cluster.

Removing a service from the cluster

Removing a service from a cluster is a very easy operation using Cloudera Manager. The following are the steps to remove a service from the cluster:

1. Navigate to the Cloudera Manager's **Home** screen. For this demonstration, let's remove the Hive service from the cluster.

2. Click on the drop-down button for the Hive service as shown in the following screenshot and select **Stop** to stop the Hive service:

3. Once the service has stopped, click on the drop-down button for the Hive service and select **Delete** to delete the service as shown in the following screenshot:

4. A pop-up message to confirm the deletion of service is displayed as shown in the following screenshot. Click on **Delete** to confirm the action.

5. Once confirmed, the service is deleted from the cluster and the service will not be visible in the list of services.

Role management in Cloudera Manager

Cloudera Manager uses **roles** to define the configuration of different hosts in a cluster. Each role will have a certain set of properties and configurations defined that can be applied to a node in the cluster. The role applied to a node will define the different Hadoop services that will run on that specific node.

The following is the list of a few roles applied to a host by Cloudera Manager:

- **Balancer**: This role is responsible for balancing the blocks across the different nodes on the cluster
- **DataNode**: This role defines all the configurations required to start a datanode on the host
- **NameNode**: This role defines all the configurations required to start a namenode on the host
- **SecondaryNameNode**: This role defines all the configurations required to start a secondary namenode on the host
- **JobTracker**: This role defines all the configurations required to start a jobtracker on the host
- **TaskTracker**: This role defines all the configurations required to start a tasktracker on the host

Adding a role instance to a host

To add a role instance to a host, navigate to **Hosts** from the Cloudera Manager toolbar. You should see a screen as shown in the following screenshot:

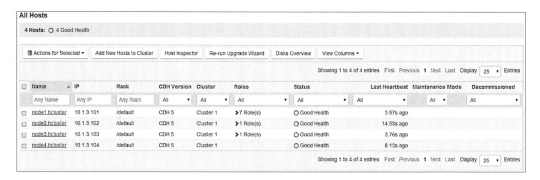

As you can see, the `node4.hcluster` host does not have any roles assigned to it. Let's say that we want the `node4.hcluster` host to run datanode and tasktracker daemons. To do this, we need to add the DataNode and TaskTracker roles to this host.

Adding a DataNode role to a host

The following are the steps to add the DataNode role to a host:

1. Navigate to the Cloudera Manager's **Clusters** menu and select **HDFS** as shown in the following screenshot:

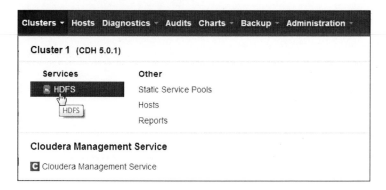

2. To add the DataNode role to the `node4.hcluster` host, select **Instances** for HDFS as shown in the following screenshot:

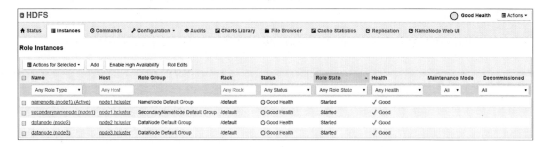

As you can see, all roles related to the **HDFS** service and the nodes to which it has been applied are listed.

3. Click on **Add** to add a new role instance. You should see the screen to add a role instance as shown in the following screenshot:

4. Click on **Select hosts** under the **DataNode** section and select **Custom...** as shown in the following screenshot:

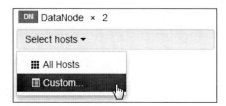

5. Next, you should see the host selection screen as shown in the following screenshot:

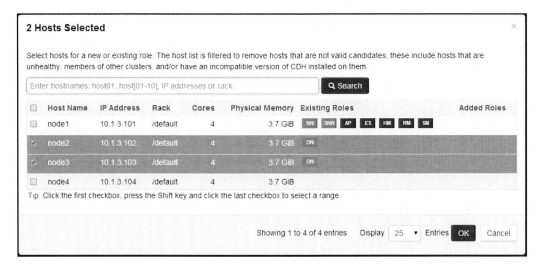

6. Select **node4** and click on **OK**.

7. Click on **Continue** on the next screen to bring up the **Review Changes** screen as shown in the following screenshot:

8. Click on **Finish** to complete the steps of adding the DataNode role. You should see the **Role Instances** screen with the newly added DataNode role as shown in the following screenshot:

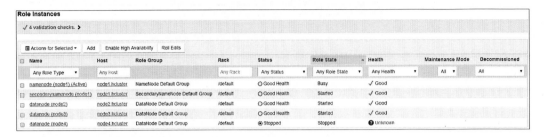

9. To start the DataNode role, check the checkbox for the **datanode (node4)** item, click on the **Actions for Selected** menu button and select **Start** as shown in the following screenshot:

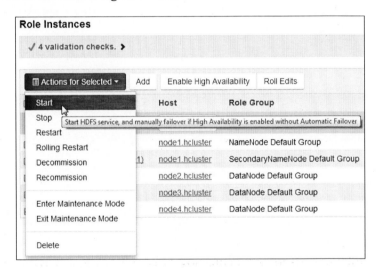

10. You should see a dialog box as shown in the following screenshot. Click on **Start** to start the datanode.

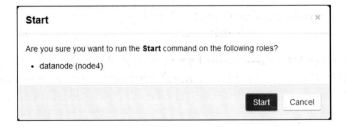

11. The datanode should start successfully as shown in the following screenshot:

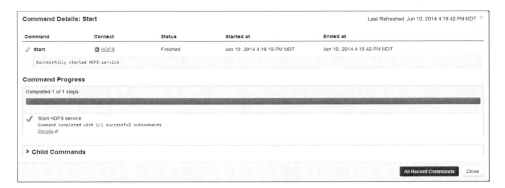

Adding a TaskTracker role to a host

The following are the steps to add the TaskTracker role to a host:

1. The TaskTracker role is part of the **MapReduce** service. Navigate to the Cloudera Manager's **Clusters** menu and select the **Instances** tab as shown in the following screenshot:

2. Click on **Add** to add a new role instance. You should see the screen to add a role instance as shown in the following screenshot:

3. Click on **Select hosts** under the **TaskTracker** section and select **Custom...**
   as shown in the following screenshot:

4. On the next screen, select **node4** as shown in the following screenshot and
   click on **OK**:

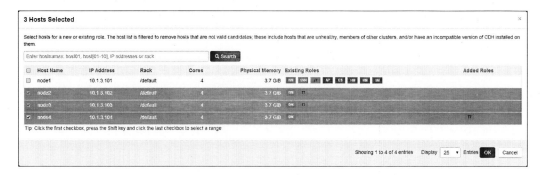

5. On the next screen, click on **Continue** to bring up the **Review Changes**
   screen as shown in the following screenshot. Click on the **Finish** button.

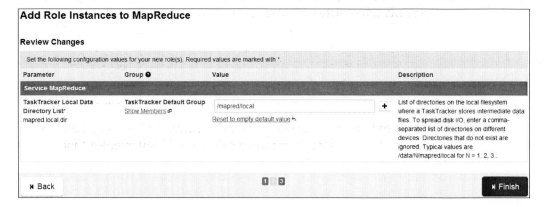

6. To start the TaskTracker role on this node, select the checkbox for **tasktracker (node4)**, click on the **Actions for Selected** menu button and click on **Start** as shown in the following screenshot:

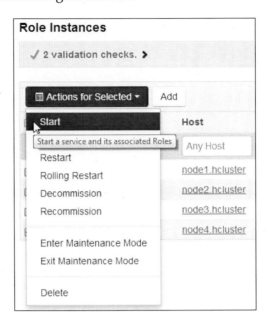

Using the preceding mentioned steps, we have successfully added the DataNode and TaskTracker roles to `node4.hcluster`. Similarly, you could add any role you want to the nodes of a cluster managed by Cloudera Manager.

Managing hosts using Cloudera Manager

Cloudera Manager makes it very simple to add and remove hosts in a cluster. All host management operations in Cloudera Manager are done from the **Hosts** screen. In this section, we will go through the steps of adding and removing hosts on the cluster.

Adding a new host

The following are the steps to add a new host to the cluster. For this demonstration, we will be adding a new node, `node4.hcluster`, to our cluster:

1. Navigate to the **Hosts** screen from the Cloudera Manager toolbar. You should see all the hosts that are part of the cluster as shown in the following screenshot:

2. Click on the **Add New Hosts to Cluster** button to add a new host. The **Add Hosts Wizard** screen, as shown in the following screenshot, is displayed. Click on **Continue**.

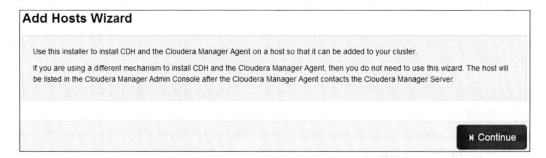

3. A search box, as shown in the following screenshot, is displayed. Type in `node4.hcluster` and click on the **Search** button to search for the `node4.hcluster` host.

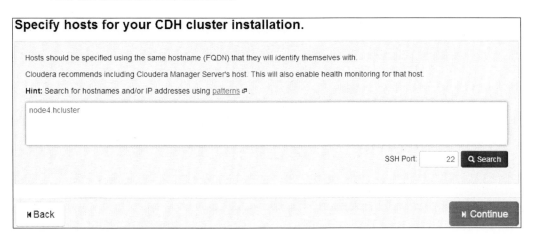

4. The search results should display the `node4.hcluster` host:

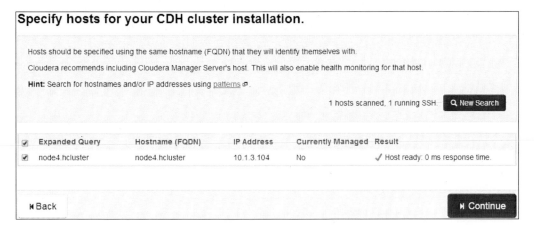

Check the checkbox to select the host and click on **Continue**.

5. Next, select **Matched release for this Cloudera Manager Server** as the repository, click on **Continue**:

6. Next, you will be prompted to configure Java encryption as shown in the following screenshot. For now, we can skip this configuration and click on **Continue**:

7. Provide the `root` user credentials for the new host and click on **Continue**:

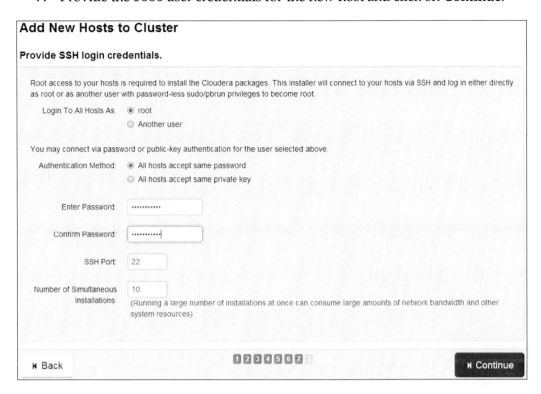

8. The next screen, as shown in the following screenshot, starts the installation of the packages required to add the host to the cluster. Once the installation is complete, click on **Continue**.

9. The next screen starts the installation of parcels on the node. Once the parcels are installed, click on **Continue**.

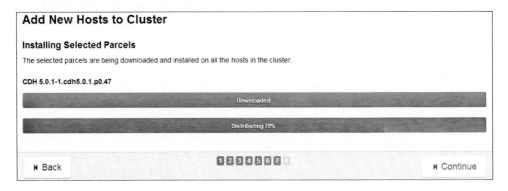

10. The next screen, as shown in the following screenshot, inspects the host for correctness. Once the inspection is complete, click on **Continue**.

11. Next, select the template to apply to the new host. Select **None** for no template as shown in the following screenshot and click on **Continue**:

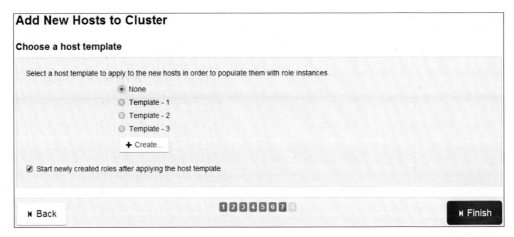

12. A message is displayed indicating successful addition of the new host:

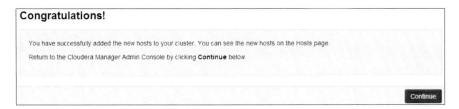

13. Click on **Continue** to complete the addition of the new host. You should now see the newly added host as part of the list of hosts as shown in the following screenshot:

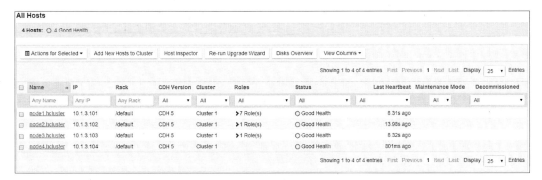

Removing an existing host

The following are the steps to remove a host from a cluster:

1. Navigate to the **Hosts** screen from the Cloudera Manager toolbar.

2. Let's say that we need to remove the `node4.hcluster` host from the cluster. Select the host, `node4.hcluster`, as shown in the following screenshot:

3. As you can see, there are two roles associated with the host: the DataNode and TaskTracker roles. Before we remove the host, we need to decommission these roles from the host.

4. Click on the **Actions for Selected** button and click on **Decommission** from the menu as shown in the following screenshot:

You will be prompted to confirm the action as shown in the following screenshot:

Click on **Confirm** to stop all the roles running on the selected host.

5. Next, we need to delete the host. Before we delete the host, we need to stop the `cloudera-scm-agent` service as the `root` user, from `node4.hcluster` using the following command:

```
$ service cloudera-scm-agent stop
```

6. Next, switch back to the **Hosts** screen and select `node4.hcluster`. Click on the **Actions for Selected** button and select **Delete** to delete the host from the cluster.

Managing multiple clusters with Cloudera Manager

Organizations could have multiple teams and each team could have a dedicated cluster. Cloudera Manager provides a feature to manage multiple clusters efficiently. In this section, we will walk through the following steps to configure a second cluster running CDH:

1. Navigate to the **Home** page and click on the drop-down button in the **Status** section. Select **Add Cluster** as shown in the following screenshot:

2. You will be prompted to search for the nodes for the new cluster as shown in the following screenshot:

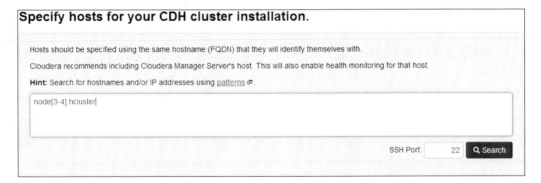

For this demonstration, let's add node3.hcluster and node4.hcluster as hosts for the new cluster. Here I am using a pattern to search for node3. hcluster and node4.hcluster. Type in the pattern or enter the hostnames in the search box and click on the **Search** button.

3. Select the `node3.hcluster` and `node4.hcluster` hosts as shown in the following screenshot. Click on **Continue**.

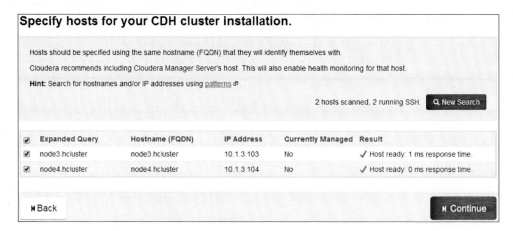

4. Select the repository for the new cluster as shown in the following screenshot and click on **Continue**:

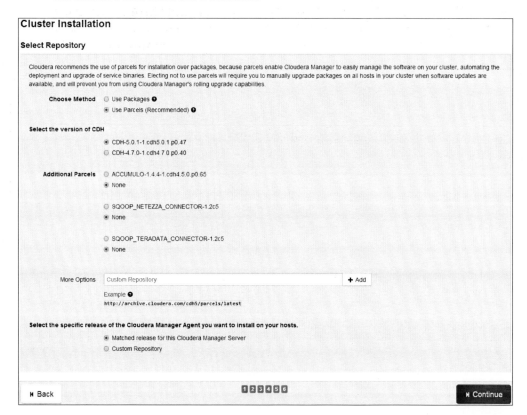

5. Next, you will be prompted to configure Java encryption as shown in the following screenshot. For now, we can skip this configuration and click on **Continue**.

6. Next, provide the `root` password for the new host/hosts as shown in the following screenshot. Click on **Continue**.

7. The next screen displays the cluster installation progress:

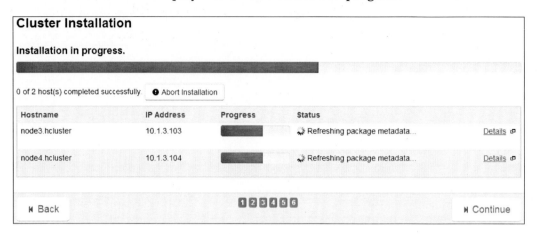

Once the installation completes, click on **Continue**.

8. The next screen installs the parcels for the hosts on the new cluster. The following is the screenshot of the parcel installation progress:

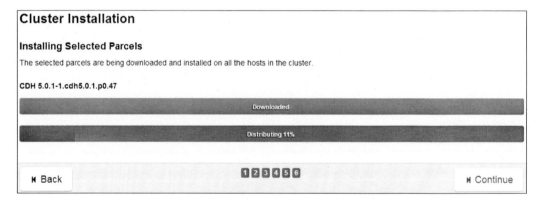

Once the parcel installation completes, click on **Continue**.

9. The next screen will inspect the newly added hosts. On successful completion of inspection, click on **Finish** to select the services for the new cluster as shown in the following screenshot:

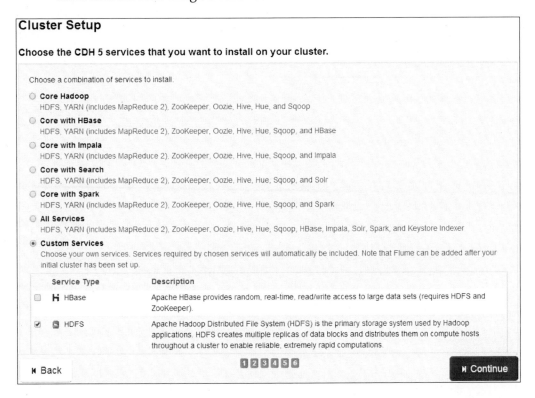

Select the services you would like to install on the new cluster and click on **Continue**. Here, **HDFS** has been selected as the service for the new cluster.

10. The next screen will prompt you to customize role assignments as shown in the following screenshot. Click on **Continue**.

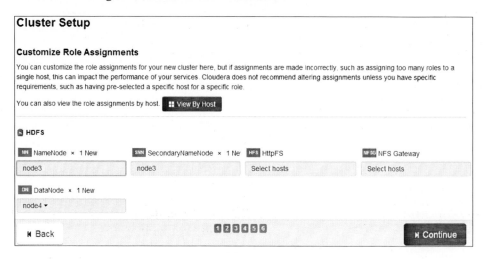

11. The next screen will prompt you to review the default configurations. Once you are done reviewing, click on **Continue**.

12. The next screen will display the **Cluster Setup** progress as shown in the following screenshot:

13. Once the installation completes, click on **Continue**. You should see a message as shown in the following screenshot on successful completion:

14. Click on **Finish**. You will be forwarded to the **Home** screen and you should see two clusters listed as shown in the following screenshot:

 For demonstration purposes, only two hosts were added as part of the new cluster—**Cluster 2**. In real production environments, several hosts would be added as part of a cluster.

Rebalancing a Hadoop cluster from Cloudera Manager

The Balancer tool available in Hadoop is used to balance the data blocks across all the datanodes when a new datanode is added or when an existing datanode reaches full capacity.

Adding the Balancer service to the cluster

Before you can rebalance a cluster, we need to add the balancer service.
The following are the steps to add the Balancer service:

1. Navigate to the **Clusters** menu and select **HDFS**.

2. Click on the **Instances** tab and select **Add** to bring up the **Customize Role Assignments** screen as shown in the following screenshot:

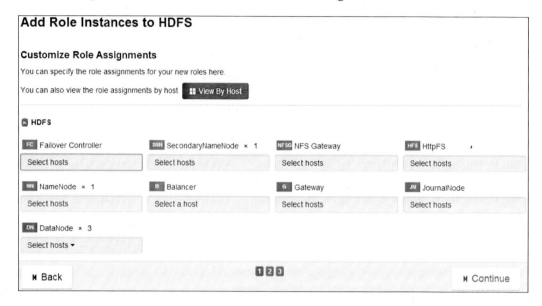

3. Click on **Select a host** for the **Balancer** section to bring up the host selection screen as shown in the following screenshot. Select a host and click on **OK**. Here I have selected **node4**.

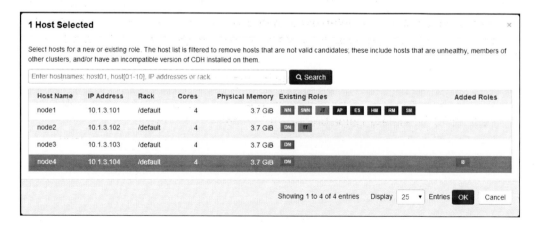

4. In the next screen, click on **Continue**. You should now see the Balancer service added, as shown in the following screenshot:

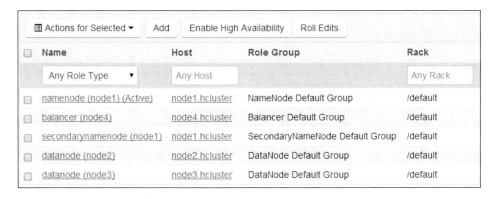

Rebalancing the cluster

Once the Balancer service is installed successfully, you can perform the rebalancing operation. The following are the steps to perform the rebalancing operation from Cloudera Manager:

1. Navigate to the **Clusters** menu and select **HDFS**.

2. Navigate to the **Instances** tab and click on the **Balancer** service from the list of services to navigate to the **balancer** screen as shown in the following screenshot:

3. Click on the **Actions** button and click on **Rebalance** as shown in the following screenshot:

4. You will be asked to confirm the action as shown in the following screenshot:

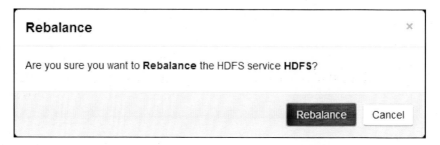

5. Click on **Rebalance** to start the rebalancing operation. On successful completion, the data blocks should be balanced across the datanodes on the cluster and you should see a message like the one shown in the following screenshot:

Summary

In this chapter, we covered several cluster management operations such as adding and removing services, managing roles, adding and removing hosts in a cluster, and rebalancing a cluster.

In the next chapter, we will study the different monitoring and troubleshooting techniques required to deal with issues arising in a Hadoop cluster.

8

Cluster Monitoring Using Events and Alerts

Every administrator will have to monitor the health of their clusters and will want to be notified of issues before they turn out to be major problems. There are several tools and techniques available within Cloudera Manager to monitor a Hadoop cluster. In this chapter, we will cover the following topics:

- Monitoring Hadoop services from Cloudera Manager
- Understanding events and alerts in Cloudera Manager

Monitoring a Hadoop cluster is a complex process as there are several services that interact with each other over the network. All of these components need to be actively monitored to identify and pinpoint the root cause for any issue that occurs. Cloudera Manager is a comprehensive cluster management application that provides a host of tools to monitor a Hadoop cluster.

Monitoring Hadoop services from Cloudera Manager

To monitor Hadoop services from Cloudera Manager, log in to Cloudera Manager and navigate to the **Home** screen. The **Home** screen lists all the services configured within the cluster as shown in the following screenshot:

The status of the services can be in any of the following states:

- **Good Health:** This is indicated by a green color
- **Concerning Health**: This is indicated by an orange color
- **Bad Heath**: This is indicated by a red color

The following are the steps to investigate a health issue for a service in a cluster. Let's try to identify the reason behind the Concerning Health status for the HDFS service.

1. Click on the Concerning Health (orange dot) status for the HDFS service. You should see the **Health Tests** section for the HDFS service as shown in the following screenshot:

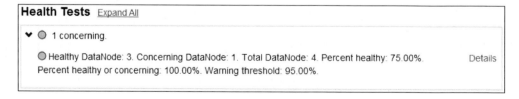

2. As you can see in the preceding screenshot, the **Health Tests** section gives details about the concern. From the message, we now know that one of the four datanodes have a Concerning Health status.

3. To get further information on a health test, click on the **Details** link to bring up the description as shown in the following screenshot:

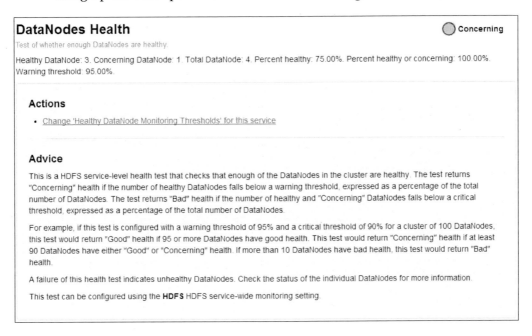

DataNodes Health   ○ Concerning

Test of whether enough DataNodes are healthy.

Healthy DataNode: 3. Concerning DataNode: 1. Total DataNode: 4. Percent healthy: 75.00%. Percent healthy or concerning: 100.00%. Warning threshold: 95.00%.

Actions

- Change 'Healthy DataNode Monitoring Thresholds' for this service

Advice

This is a HDFS service-level health test that checks that enough of the DataNodes in the cluster are healthy. The test returns "Concerning" health if the number of healthy DataNodes falls below a warning threshold, expressed as a percentage of the total number of DataNodes. The test returns "Bad" health if the number of healthy and "Concerning" DataNodes falls below a critical threshold, expressed as a percentage of the total number of DataNodes.

For example, if this test is configured with a warning threshold of 95% and a critical threshold of 90% for a cluster of 100 DataNodes, this test would return "Good" health if 95 or more DataNodes have good health. This test would return "Concerning" health if at least 90 DataNodes have either "Good" or "Concerning" health. If more than 10 DataNodes have bad health, this test would return "Bad" health.

A failure of this health test indicates unhealthy DataNodes. Check the status of the individual DataNodes for more information.

This test can be configured using the **HDFS** HDFS service-wide monitoring setting.

4. Next, navigate to the **Instances** tab for the service shown in the following screenshot:

Role Instances

✓ 4 validation checks. >

Actions for Selected ▾   Add   Enable High Availability   Roll Edits

	Name	Host	Role Group	Rack	Status	Role State ▲	Health	Maintenance Mode	Decommissioned
	Any Role Type ▾	Any Host		Any Rack	Any Status ▾	Any Role State ▾	Any Health ▾	All ▾	All ▾
☐	datanode (node1)	node1.hcluster	DataNode Default Group	/default	◎ Concerning Health	Started	⚠ Concerning		
☐	namenode (node1) (Active)	node1.hcluster	NameNode Default Group	/default	○ Good Health	Started	✓ Good		
☐	secondarynamenode (node1)	node1.hcluster	SecondaryNameNode Default Group	/default	○ Good Health	Started	✓ Good		
☐	datanode (node2)	node2.hcluster	DataNode Default Group	/default	○ Good Health	Started	✓ Good		
☐	datanode (node3)	node3.hcluster	DataNode Default Group	/default	○ Good Health	Started	✓ Good		
☐	datanode (node4)	node4.hcluster	DataNode Default Group	/default	○ Good Health	Started	✓ Good		

5. Click on the datanode with the concerning health, in this case, `node1.hcluster`. You should see the results of the **Health Tests** section for the node in the following screenshot:

6. As shown in the preceding screenshot, the message indicates that swapping is causing the concerning health of the datanode. Swapping occurs when a process uses more memory than is available on the machine. Excessive or persistent swapping could be an indication that there is insufficient RAM on the node.

7. Adding RAM requires the node to be turned off. In some cases, where the node is a virtual machine, RAM can be added even with the node running. Allocate or add more RAM as required to the node.

8. After adding RAM to the node, we see that all health tests have been successfully passed, as shown in the following screenshot:

Health Tests Collapse All

- ✔ ○ 11 good.

- ○ Space free on data volumes: 27.2 GiB. Capacity of data volumes: 40.4 GiB. Percentage of capacity free: 67.38%. — Details
- ○ This DataNode is connected to its NameNode(s). — Details
- ○ The DataNode has 0 volume failure(s). — Details
- ○ The DataNode has 157 blocks. — Details
- ○ This role's status is as expected. The role is started. — Details
- ○ This role encountered 0 unexpected exit(s) in the previous 5 minute(s). — Details
- ○ Open file descriptors: 332. File descriptor limit: 32,768. Percentage in use: 1.01%. — Details
- ○ This role's log directory (/var/log/hadoop-hdfs) is on a filesystem with more than 10.0 GiB of its space free. — Details
- ○ The health of this role's host is good. — Details
- ○ The web server of this role is responding with metrics. The most recent collection took 32 millisecond(s). — Details
- ○ Average time spent in garbage collection was 0 second(s) (0.00%) per minute over the previous 5 minute(s). — Details

To view the logfile for the service, you can click on the **Log File** hyperlink on the **Status** tab of the service as shown in the following screenshot:

The **Log Details** page displays the datanode logfile in a columnar format as shown in the following screenshot:

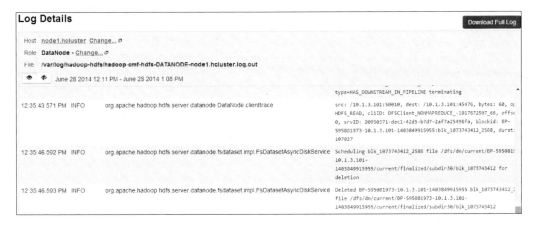

You can download the entire logfile using the **Download Full Log** button. The logfile can also be viewed directly by logging into the node and navigating to the `/var/log/hadoop-hdfs/` location of the respective node.

Understanding events and alerts

Events are records of certain occurrences in the system and are very useful to track the different operations running on the cluster. Several events are configured by default when Cloudera Manager is installed.

All events in the cluster are managed by the Event Server component of Cloudera Manager. To view the events, navigate to **Diagnostics | Events** from the Cloudera Manager toolbar. The following is the screenshot of the **Events** page:

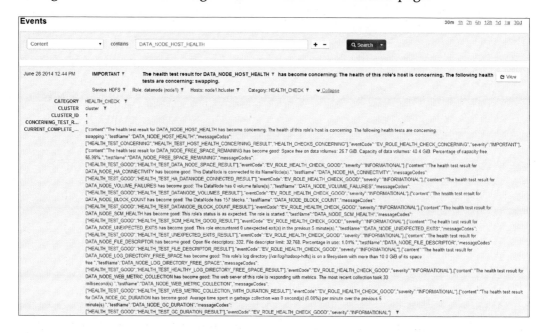

The preceding screenshot shows one event for the HDFS service that is part of the `node1.hcuster` host and the **datanode (node1)** role. The screenshot also shows the details of the alert that is displayed when you click on the **Expand** link. To close the details, you can use the **Collapse** link.

Search filters can also be applied to perform more advanced searches. Click on the **Add a filter** hyperlink to add filters as shown in the following screenshot:

To open up the datanode instance, click on the **View** button. The following screenshot shows the **datanode (node1)** instance that corresponds to the event:

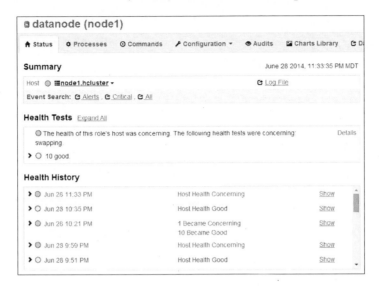

To view the logfile for this datanode, that is, **datanode (node1)**, click on the **Log File** link to open the **Logs** search screen as shown in the following screenshot:

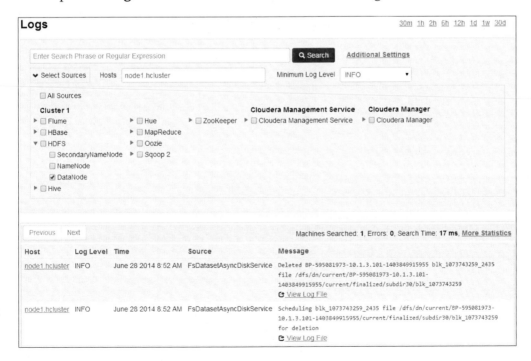

Configuring events and alerts

Alerts are messages that are configured to be triggered by an event. Alerts are configured to inform the occurrence of events that need special attention.

The following are the steps to configure an event. For this example, we will configure an event to monitor HDFS free space:

1. Navigate to the **Home** page from the Cloudera Manager toolbar.
2. Select the HDFS service to navigate to the HDFS service details page.
3. Navigate to **Configuration | View and Edit** and select the **Monitoring** section.
4. Click on **Service-Wide** to display all the configuration parameters for the HDFS service as shown in the following screenshot:

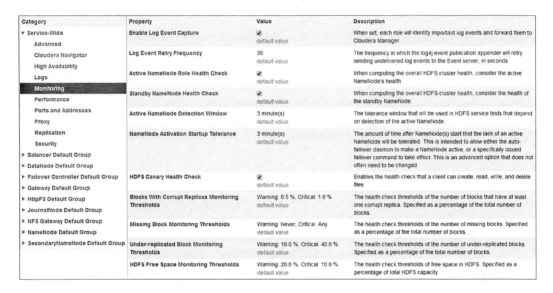

5. The default value configured for the **HDFS Free Space Monitoring Thresholds** property are **20.0%** and **10.0%** for the **Warning** and **Critical** events, respectively. This means that a **Warning** event will be triggered when the free space on HDFS reaches 20 percent and a **Critical** event will be triggered when the HDFS free space reaches 10 percent.

For this illustration, let's update the values **25%** and **20%** for the **Warning** and **Critical** events respectively, as shown in the following screenshot:

6. Once done, save the changes by clicking on the **Save Changes** button.

7. Now, whenever the free space on HFDS goes below 25 percent, a **Warning** event will be generated. Similarly, if the free space on HDFS goes below 20 percent, a **Critical** event will be generated.

   The following screenshot shows the event generated when the free space on HDFS is below the set critical threshold of 20 percent:

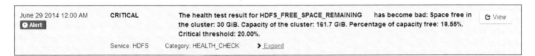

   You will observe that the event is labeled as **Alert**. This is because the HDFS service is configured to alert us if the service's status becomes bad.

8. To see more details for this alert, click on the **Expand** link. You should see additional details as shown in the following screenshot:

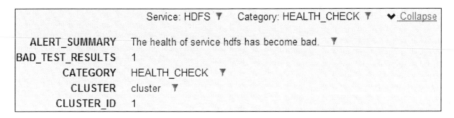

9. To see the list of all alerts configured, navigate to the **Administration** menu of the Cloudera Manager toolbar and select **Alerts**. The **Alerts** page is displayed as shown in the following screenshot:

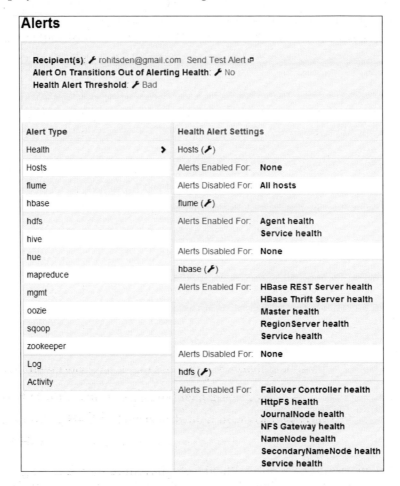

The following alert types can be configured from Cloudera Manager:

- ° **Health**: The properties configured within this section are to do with the health of the individual services running within the cluster.
- ° **Log**: The properties configured within this section are to do with alerts to be generated for certain types of log messages found in the logs of the individual services.
- ° **Activity**: The properties configured within this section are to do with alerts to be generated by the activity monitor that monitors jobs that fail or perform slowly.

Configuring the alert delivery by an e-mail

Administrators would want to be alerted of certain events by e-mail rather than having to check the **Events** page for alerts and events. The following are the steps to configure the alert delivery by an e-mail:

1. Navigate to the **Home** screen from the Cloudera Manager toolbar.

2. Click on the **Cloudera Management Service** tab to open up the **Cloudera Management Service** details page and navigate to **Configuration | View and Edit** as shown in the following screenshot:

3. Select the **Alert Publisher Default Group** section as shown in the following screenshot:

4. Update the **Alerts: Mail Server Hostname** property to the IP address or the hostname of your SMTP server.

5. Update the **Alerts: Mail Message Recipients** property to the e-mail ID or a comma-separated list of e-mail IDs to whom the alerts need to be sent, as shown in the following screenshot:

6. Click on **Save Changes** to save the configuration changes.

7. Restart the Cloudera Manager service for the changes to take effect.

8. We are done with the configurations and will now start receiving alerts via e-mail. A sample alert e-mail is shown in the following screenshot:

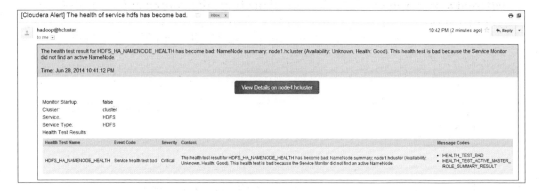

 In this chapter, we only covered the basics of monitoring, events, and alerts. Cloudera documentation provides an in-depth description of the various options available for monitoring the entire cluster and can be found at http://www.cloudera.com/content/cloudera-content/cloudera-docs/CM5/latest/Cloudera-Manager-Diagnostics-Guide/Cloudera-Manager-Diagnostics-Guide.html.

Summary

In this chapter, we walked you through the steps to monitor Hadoop services using Cloudera Manager. Next, we configured events and alerts and also set up alert delivery by e-mail.

In the next chapter, you will learn the importance of backups and the different backup options provided by Cloudera Manager.

Configuring Backups

9

As Hadoop clusters mature, the data residing in them grows, and maintaining a copy of the data turns out to be an important responsibility of a Hadoop administrator. Backing up data from a distributed environment is a challenge due to its ever increasing volume. Setting up backup operations is an important step towards restoring data in case of entire cluster failures. This chapter discusses the various backup and data protection options and will cover the following topics:

- Understanding backups
- Understanding HDFS backups
- Using the **distributed copy (DistCp)**
- Configuring backups using Cloudera Manager

Understanding backups

Systems that deal with information or data, whether standalone or distributed, have to plan for disasters and complete system failures. Configuring and setting up backup policies for systems is an integral part of any disaster recovery plan. A backup is a copy of the data in use, which is also sometimes referred to as an archive. In the case of failures leading to data loss, the copy is used to restore data.

Backups, depending on the days of retention, demand vast amount of data storage. However, in the case of data storage media used for backups, the read and write speeds are not of much importance. Organizations procure more reliable storage media and do not worry about the read/write speeds as data from backup storage media is only read from in the case of disasters.

Types of backups

There are several types of backup policies that can be considered before including them in the disaster recovery plan of your organization. This decision is solely based on the organizations, requirements on how they would want to manage their data. The following are a few of the different types of backups:

- **The full backup**: A full backup involves archiving all data from the source location to the target backup location. Almost all backup solutions start with the full backup first and subsequently tend to use the other backup methods. Recurring schedules for full backups are only done on smaller amounts of data. Performing full backups on every schedule for large volumes of data is not advisable as such backups can be very time consuming and would demand larger storage spaces.

- **The incremental backup**: Incremental backups involve the archiving of only the changes made to the data since the last backup. The first incremental backup is preceded by a full backup and subsequently when data is changed or added, only the data that has changed/added is backed up. Restoring data from incrementally backed up data can be slower as it involves the process of first restoring the initial full backup and subsequently applying the incremental restores on top.

- **The differential backup**: The differential backup involves archiving only the changes made to the data since the last full backup. The important term to note here is **full backup**. This is what sets differential backups apart from incremental backups. Restoring from differential backups is faster than restoring from incremental backups.

- **The mirror backup**: Mirror backups involve the duplication of every operation in the source location to the target location. So in this case, when data is deleted in the source, it is also deleted from the target backup location, maintaining a mirror image of the original data. Using this type of backup could result in loss of data from the backup location in the case of an accidental deletion from the source location.

Types of storage media for backups

There are different types of storage media that can be used for backups. The following is a list of commonly used storage media:

- **Hard disks**: Hard disks are the most commonly used storage media for backups as the cost per byte has come down over the years. They are found with several speeds and sizes. Some hard disks are manufactured with a design for backup. With hard disks, it is important to note that they are not particularly reliable for data storage with retention periods that span over several years.

- **Optical storage**: Removable and portable media such as recordable **compact discs (CD)**, **digital video discs (DVD)**, and **Blu-ray Discs (BD)** are also being used for backups. These are particularly used to store small amounts of data and are not used to back up data from environments such as large data clusters.

- **Tape drives**: Tapes are probably the oldest forms of backup storage media still in use today in many organizations. This is mainly because of the low cost per byte they offer. However, this is slowly changing as hard disks are now being used to store data.

Using cloud services for backups

In recent years, there have been several cloud service offerings that provide storage space on the cloud to back up an organization's critical data. This eliminates the need for organizations to set up a different physical site to back up their data. Services such as Amazon's AWS provides storage as a service that can be accessed over the Internet. They provide several disaster recovery architectures that make it easy to set up a backup site on the cloud. More information on Amazon's offering can be found at http://aws.amazon.com/disaster-recovery/.

Understanding HDFS backups

Data volumes in Hadoop clusters range from terabytes to petabytes, and deciding what data to back up from such clusters is an important decision. A disaster recovery plan for Hadoop clusters needs to be formulated right at the cluster planning stages. The organization needs to identify the datasets they want to back up and plan backup storage requirements accordingly.

Backup schedules also need to be considered when designing a backup solution. The larger the data that needs to be backed up, the more time-consuming the activity. It would be more efficient if backups could be performed during a window when there is the least amount of activity on the cluster. This not only helps the backup commands to run efficiently, but also ensures data consistency of the datasets being backed up. Knowing the possible schedules of the data infusion to HDFS in advance helps you to better plan and schedule backup solutions for Hadoop clusters.

The following are some of the important data sources that need to be protected against data loss:

- **The namenode metadata**: The namenode metadata contains all the location of all the files in the HDFS.
- **The Hive metastore**: The Hive metastore contains the metadata for all Hive tables and partitions.
- **HBase RegionServer data**: This contains the information of all the HBase regions.
- **Application configuration files**: This comprises the important configuration files required to configure Apache Hadoop. For example, `core-site.xml`, `yarn-site.xml`, and `hdfs-site.xml`.

Data protection in Hadoop clusters is important as clusters are prone to data corruption, hardware failures, and accidental data deletion. In rare cases, a data center catastrophe could also lead to entire data loss.

Using the distributed copy (DistCp)

Distributed copy (DistCp) is a Hadoop utility used to copy data in parallel within and between clusters. It uses Hadoop's MapReduce to perform the copy operation. DistCp is the most widely used data transfer tool in Hadoop clusters. For example:

```
$ hadoop distcp hdfs://namenode1/src hdfs://namenode2/dest
```

The preceding command would copy the `src` folder and all its contents from the cluster managed by `namenode1` to the cluster managed by `namenode2` as the `dest` folder. DistCp, by default, does not overwrite the files at the target location and skips copying them if the files already exists. However, files can be forced to be overwritten using the `overwrite` flag.

There are several options that can be used along with the Hadoop `distcp` command and the details of these options can be found at `http://www.cloudera.com/content/cloudera-content/cloudera-docs/CDH5/latest/CDH5-Installation-Guide/cdh5ig_distcp_data_cluster_migrate.html`.

Configuring backups using Cloudera Manager

Cloudera provides a licensed feature for backups. From the Cloudera Manager toolbar, navigate to the **Backup** menu to find the backup features, as shown in the following screenshot:

Configuring HDFS replication

Replications allow an administrator to replicate data from one cluster to another. The following are the steps to configure a schedule for HDFS replication:

1. Navigate to **Backups** | **Replications** to bring up the screen shown in the following screenshot:

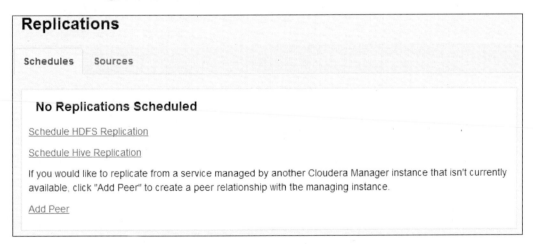

2. Under the **Schedules** tab, schedules for HDFS replications and Hive replication can be configured. Click on **Schedule HDFS Replication** to bring up the screen as shown in the following screenshot:

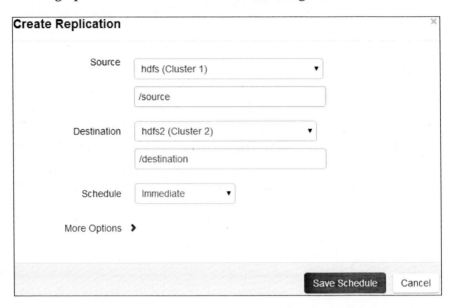

3. As you can see in the preceding screenshot, the **Source**, **Destination**, and **Schedule** fields for HDFS replication can be configured. In this configuration, we have configured a schedule to replicate data from the source folder from HDFS in **hdfs (Cluster 1)** to the destination folder of HDFS in **hdfs2 (Cluster 2)**.

As part of the schedule configuration, there are three types of options available as shown in the following screenshot:

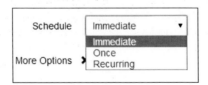

4. The **Immediate** option schedules the HDFS replication to start immediately on saving the schedule.

5. On selecting the **Once** option, the start time of the HDFS replication can be set as shown in the following screenshot:

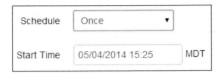

6. The **Recurring** option provides the ability to set a recurring schedule for HDFS replication as shown in the following screenshot:

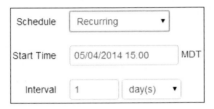

A few more configuration options are available and they are visible on selecting the **More Options** link. The following screenshot that shows the first half of the different options available:

The following screenshot shows the second half of the different options available:

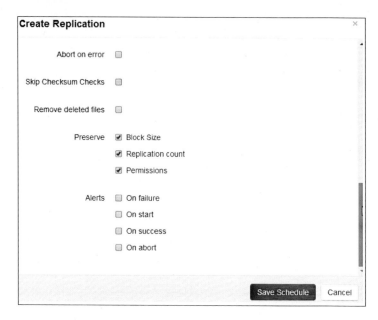

A description of each of these configuration parameters is available at `http://www.cloudera.com/content/cloudera-content/cloudera-docs/CM5/latest/Cloudera-Backup-Disaster-Recovery/cm5bdr_hdfs_replication.html`.

7. Once the configuration is complete, click on **Save Schedule** to save the schedule. A HDFS replication job can be monitored from the **Replications** screen as shown in the following screenshot:

Configuring Hive replication

Just like HDFS replication, Hive metadata replication schedules can be configured using the following steps:

1. Navigate to **Backups | Replications** from the Cloudera Manager toolbar. To configure the replication schedule for Hive, click on **Schedule Hive Replication**. You should see a dialog box as shown in the following screenshot:

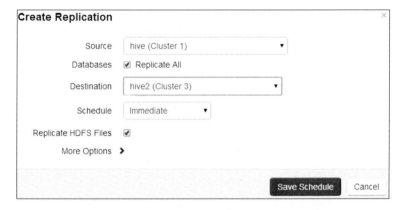

As you've seen in the preceding screenshot, we have configured the Hive replication schedule to replicate Hive metadata from **hive (Cluster 1)** to **hive2 (Cluster 3)**. The scheduling options are similar to that of HDFS replication. The following screenshot is the first half of the **More Options** section for Hive replication:

The following screenshot is the second half of the **More Options** section for Hive replication:

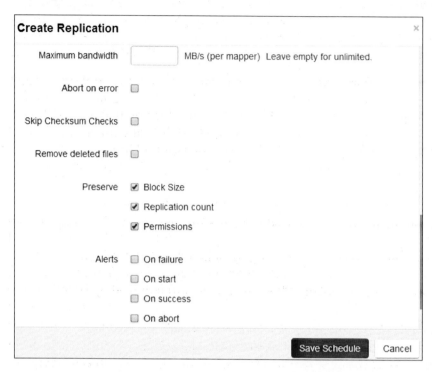

2. Once the configuration parameters are set, the schedule can be saved by clicking on the **Save Schedule** button. The Hive replication job can be monitored from the **Replications** screen as shown in the following screenshot:

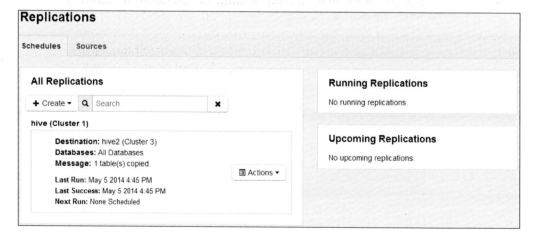

The **Sources** tab lists the different sources available for replication. The following screenshot is the **Sources** tab:

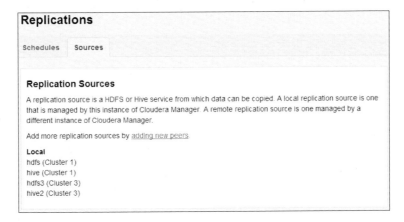

Configuring snapshots

Snapshots is a feature that allows administrators to configure paths in HDFS to be copied for the purposes of backup and data protection. The very first step before configuring a snapshot is to create a **snapshottable** path.

Enabling snapshot paths in HDFS

To set a HDFS path as snapshottable, perform the following steps:

1. Navigate to the HDFS service of the cluster where you want to set up a snapshottable path and navigate to the **File Browser** tab. Navigate to the path that needs the snapshot enabled. The following screenshot shows the **File Browser** tab of the **hdfs** service available on **Cluster 1**:

In the preceding screenshot, we is navigated to the /user/root/source path.

2. Next, click on the **Enable Snapshots** button to bring up the dialog box shown in the following screenshot:

3. Next, click on the **Enable Snapshots** button to make the `source` folder at `/user/root` snapshottable. You should see a command completion message as shown in the following screenshot:

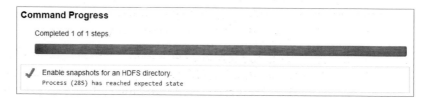

Configuring a snapshot policy

The following are the steps to create a snapshot policy for snapshottable paths on HDFS:

1. Navigate to **Backups** | **Snapshots** to bring up the screen as shown in the following screenshot:

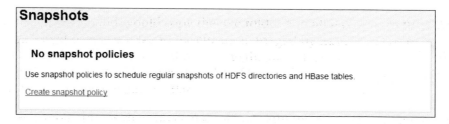

2. Next, click on the **Create snapshot policy** link to bring up the dialog box shown in the following screenshot:

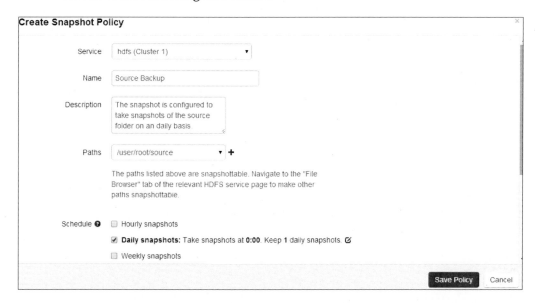

As you see in the preceding screenshot, the policy is configured to take a snapshot daily. There are few more options available under the **More Options** section as shown in the following screenshot:

3. After setting the required configuration parameters, click on **Save Policy** to save the snapshot policy. You should see the newly created snapshot as shown in the following screenshot:

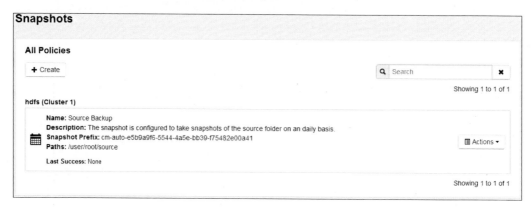

Summary

In this chapter, you understood what backups are and the different types of backups, along with the different storage media used for backups. You also learned about HDFS backups and covered the basics of using the Hadoop utility—DistCp. Next, we covered Cloudera's backup options, replication, and snapshots using Cloudera Manager.

In this book, we started out with the very basics of Hadoop and walked through the entire Cloudera distribution, covering each and every aspect of managing Hadoop clusters that run CDH and Cloudera Manager. Using the knowledge acquired from this book, you should now be ready to take up the responsibilities of a Hadoop administrator and get start managing huge Hadoop clusters.

Index

JournalNodes 96-98

K

KDC 149
KDC installation
  testing 155
KDC Server
  configuring 152-154
kerberized 151
Kerberos
  about 148
  architecture 149
  installing 148
  requirements 148
  using 147
Kerberos architecture
  about 149, 150
  authentication service component 150
  database component 150
  kerberized 151
  keys 152
  keytab 152
  principal 151
  realm 151
  secure file server, accessing 150, 151
  Ticket Granting Server component 150
  user, authenticating 150
Kerberos clients
  configuring 155
Kerberos configuration, for Apache Hadoop
  Cloudera Manager Server, configuring for
    Kerberos 158-162
  hdfs user 156
  hue user 156
  Kerberos principal, configuring for
    Cloudera Manager Server 157, 158
  mapred user 156
  oozie user 156
  yarn user 156
Kerberos installation
  clients, installing 155
  KDC installation, testing 155
  KDC Server, configuring 152-154
Kerberos principal
  configuring, for Cloudera Manager
    Server 157, 158

Kerberos screen, Administration menu 141
Key Distribution Center. *See* KDC
key pair 40
keys, Kerberos 152
keytab, Kerberos 152

L

Language screen, Administration menu 141
Leader election service, Apache
    Flume NG 62
License screen, Administration menu 141
Lightweight Directory Access Protocol
    (LDAP) 116, 140
Local Logs section, jobtracker UI
  about 51
  Job Tracker History 51
locking service, Apache Flume NG 62
Logs screen, Diagnostics menu 137
ls command 34

M

mapred.child.java.opts property 47
mapred.compress.map.output property 47
mapred.job.reuse.jvm.num.tasks
    property 47
mapred.job.tracker property 46
mapred.map.output.compression.codec
    property 47
mapred.map.tasks.speculative.execution
    property 47
mapred.output.compression.codec
    property 46
mapred.output.compression.type
    property 46
mapred.output.compress property 46
mapred.reduce.parallel.copies property 47
mapred.reduce.slowstart.completed.maps
    property 47
mapred.reduce.tasks property 47
mapred.reduce.tasks.speculative.execution
    property 47
mapred.submit.replication property 47
map, MapReduce 10
MapReduce
  about 8, 10, 39
  configuring 44-47

Decommissioning Nodes 32
DFS Remaining 31
DFS Remaining% 31
DFS Used 30
DFS Used% 31
Live Nodes 31
Non DFS Used 30
Number of Under-Replicated Blocks 32
synchronization service, Apache Flume NG 62

T

tail command 37
tape drives, storage media 215
tasktracker daemon 14-16
TaskTracker role, Cloudera Manager
about 172
adding, to host 177-179
templates tab, Host menu 136
Ticket Granting Server 150
Ticket Granting Ticket (TGT) 150
transitionToActive option 105
transitionToStandby option 105
types, backup
differential backup 214
full backup 214
incremental backup 214
mirror backup 214

U

Uniform Resource Identifier (URI) 34
user
authenticating 150
Users screen, Administration menu 141

V

value pair 40
ViewFS
about 94
configuring, for federated HDFS 94

W

workflow 66
Workflows tab, Dashboard application 74

Y

YARN
about 10, 16
job submission 17, 18
YARN cluster
about 82, 83
daemons 82
yarn user 156
Yet Another Resource Negotiator. *See* **YARN**

Z

Zippy. *See* **Snappy**
ZK Failover Controller. *See* **ZKFC service**
ZKFC component 108
ZKFC service
operations, health monitoring 108
operations, ZooKeeper-based election 109
operations, ZooKeeper session management 108
znode (ZooKeeper node) 63

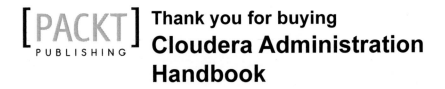

Learning Cloudera Impala

ISBN: 978-1-78328-127-5   Paperback: 150 pages

Perform interactive, real-time in-memory analytics on large amounts of data using the massive parallel processing engine Cloudera Impala

1. Step-by-step guidance to get you started with Impala on your Hadoop cluster.

2. Manipulate your data rapidly by writing proper SQL statements.

3. Explore the concepts of Impala security, administration, and troubleshooting in detail to maintain your Impala cluster.

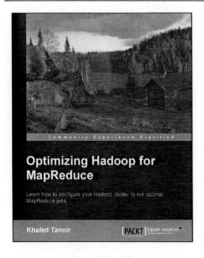

Optimizing Hadoop for MapReduce

ISBN: 978-1-78328-565-5   Paperback: 120 pages

Learn how to configure your Hadoop cluster to run optimal MapReduce jobs

1. Optimize your MapReduce job performance.

2. Identify your Hadoop cluster's weaknesses.

3. Tune your MapReduce configuration.

Please check **www.PacktPub.com** for information on our titles

[PACKT]
PUBLISHING

Big Data Analytics with R and Hadoop

ISBN: 978-1-78216-328-2   Paperback: 238 pages

Set up an integrated infrastructure of R and Hadoop to turn your data analytics into Big Data analytics

1. Write Hadoop MapReduce within R.

2. Learn data analytics with R and the Hadoop platform.

3. Handle HDFS data within R.

4. Understand Hadoop streaming with R.

5. Encode and enrich datasets into R.

Apache Solr 4 Cookbook

ISBN: 978-1-78216-132-5   Paperback: 328 pages

Over 100 recipes to make Apache Solr faster, more reliable, and return better results

1. Learn how to make Apache Solr search faster, more complete, and comprehensively scalable.

2. Solve performance, setup, configuration, analysis, and query problems in no time.

3. Get to grips with, and master, the new exciting features of Apache Solr 4.

Please check **www.PacktPub.com** for information on our titles